The ~~cosmetics~~ entrepreneur manual
The first complete book about starting a cosmetics business

written by
Davor Pavlić

2017

copyright:
Davor Pavlić

cover art sculpture:
Jasenko Đorđević, TOLDart
http://www.toldart.com/

Independently published
ISBN: 9781973447610

He has achieved success
who has lived well,
laughed often, and loved much;

who has enjoyed the trust of
pure women,

the respect of intelligent men and
the love of little children;

who has filled his niche and accomplished his task;

who has left the world better than he found it
whether by an improved poppy,
a perfect poem or a rescued soul;

who has never lacked appreciation of Earth's beauty
or failed to express it;

who has always looked for the best in others and
given them the best he had;

whose life was an inspiration;
whose memory a benediction.

Success
Bessie Anderson Stanley, 1904.

Who the book is for?

This book is for a cosmetics entrepreneur who is only starting up his or hers business. You will learn all the details of the process which takes you from your idea to your product. What you need to be, what you must be on the lookout for when dealing with laboratories, about a business plan, marketing and funding.

It will help you to become more familiar with the process of creating your own product in cooperation with a laboratory. You will get insight in the things you need to do and some hidden costs of doing business in this field.

This book is also for someone who has already started working with cosmetics, but is lacking in some areas. Maybe you want to better understand the process that is going on behind the scenes or maybe you want to explore more options of raising funds or maybe you are curious about marketing. In this book we speak about close to 40 different possibilities of marketing your products and 15 different ways of getting funds.

I do address certain attributes of a person that are beneficial for this business, but do not let that discourage you. Even if you aren't like that in nature now, many of those attributes can be acquired, trained and nurtured.

I do not address in great detail how you would be formulating your products. So, while I do believe that this book will be helpful for most of the things that are concerning the starting of the business in cosmetics and business in general, this book is not for the chemist aficionado.

Why is this book good?

While reading this book you may believe the book and the advice in it are simple at times or most of the time, but the issue is that we often skip past the simple things, so they actually tend to be quite rare in application. While, when presented, these things seem obvious, they are not that often apparent. We tend to work on figuring out these complicated things because we just don't believe that the solution can be that simple. Sometimes we convince ourselves that the reason we haven't done something is because it is too complicated and too hard to do. But it's not. So, I like to say, and I probably stole this, that simplicity is something you need to rise to, past complication.

Even so, this book does give you more information than you would usually get when asking about creating a cosmetic line, this book is about creating a cosmetics business. This book is basically a marriage between a guide to a cosmetic line and a Napoleon Hill-like book.

Foreword

Who am I and why do I think I can tell you anything about being an entrepreneur in the world of cosmetics?

My name is Davor Pavlić and I am an entrepreneur who has been on the same journey that you are on now. I have been looking for information about how to start a cosmetic line and a cosmetics company and not finding one I decided to compile some information for myself.

After some downloading of PDF documents and some bookmarking I have come to an idea to write my own manual for this. I have found some pieces of information in form of an e-book, but none of those were complete enough for me and the readers have been giving them bad reviews.

The reason I am giving myself the right to talk to you about this is because I have started from zero. I did not have an education in chemistry except from middle school and high school, I did not work in a laboratory, I did not work in the fashion industry, apart from being a photographer. I am where I am right now only because of my passion for not taking things for what they are, but what they could be – reinventing how they could be used or how they could be improved. I am emphasizing this as a positive because I want you to know that I have been through the same process you are going through now and I am writing this because it is easier to take some advice from me than from someone who has 20 years of experience, has the money to fund every experiment he or she wants. I have started with 0 funding from YouTube or some online service. Since private labelling is fairly easy I will assume that if you're reading this you will want your own products, not only change the packaging on an existing one.

This is a little bit of my story and what I found out during the reading of countless articles, books, masters and doctoral thesis, watching YouTube videos and listening to interviews that address topics mentioned in this book.

I hope you will enjoy the read and find it useful.

Author

For my mother.

Table of Contents

Introduction

The idea of entrepreneurship is a funny one. What I mean by this is that entrepreneurship not only evolved, but the whole perception of it did too. If you were to say a few decades ago that you were an entrepreneur you would have been looked upon as a failure, someone who couldn't get a job. Today, being an entrepreneur, at least a successful one, is looked upon with admiration and some romantic ideas of this prestigious role. We admire people like Mark Cuban, Sir Richard Branson, Warren Buffet... And rightfully so.

So, following these people through social and other media now we might want to become like them. Just as we used to (and still do sometimes) aspire to become great athletes, singers, etc., we are now presented with one more opportunity, to engage in the sport of business, as Mark Cuban likes to refer to it. And given that social media isn't reserved only for people, but also companies, we are exposed to the new marketing strategies and new and emerging companies are demanding our attention.

Some of these newer companies are in the fields of technology, apparel, but some are in the field of cosmetics. Cosmetics are now not reserved only for these corporate giants and the smaller companies are taking part of the market. This has further incentivized people to think about what they can and want to do and eventually start a business, which has sometimes lead to great ideas and great products. Sometimes this is a business with natural cosmetics, which you could "cook" yourself, sometimes it's a cooperation with a professional laboratory.

Sadly, social media being what it is, it is only showing the best moments of the social and business life of CEO's and companies, so unaware people are often taunted to try and do something similar themselves, only to be caught unaware of the actual ups and downs that being an entrepreneur brings along.

Hopefully, this book will help correct some of the perceptions and introduce to you some other issues you will need to think about if you want to run a successful business, not only how to contact a laboratory. So let's try to tackle some of these topics.

1 What YOU need to have

In everything that you do there are always certain things or attributes or something that will be required of you in order to prevail in that business. The recipe is hardly universal, that is why the list can go on and on and we could write a book called "100 things you need to be to be an entrepreneur".

I do not believe that you need to be 100 things or even 50 things to be an entrepreneur. How do you even recognize an entrepreneur? Usually we believe that an entrepreneur is a person who owns and runs a business, which isn't true. At least not entirely. An entrepreneur could be anyone. Even if you are "only" an employee, you could be an entrepreneur. Just by improving your business environment, the effectiveness of your work… Whatever you can do to make something better for yourself, people you work with or for or your customers, is entrepreneurial.

Sometimes people will tell you there is a definite number of steps you need to take – there isn't. You may need to make two steps more or one step less, you can never know. Also, there is no definite order. But most importantly, people will usually start these steps by telling you how you need a company. You do…n't. OK, yes, you need a company. But unless you have one already, you don't want to make this your first step. Why start a company if you don't have a laboratory to work with or money to fund all your products or at least prospects of getting money? You will eventually need a registered entity with a bank account and everything that follows, but cover your basis.

But let's start with something easier first. Following the inscription on the oracle of Delphi, first you need to get to know yourself.

1.1 What you need to be

Without making you read the whole book I will tell you which attributes you need to have to succeed in this and in many other lines of business.
1. You need to be curious,
2. You need to be driven and motivated by something,
3. You need to have a desire to work in this field,
4. You need to want to make a difference, not only money,
5. You need to be creative,
6. You need to be at least somewhat communicative,
7. You need to be focused,

8. You need to divide tasks,
9. You need to not be afraid.

You need to be curious. Even as a child I loved all sorts of chemistry. Or whatever I considered to be chemistry at that young age. This continued throughout the middle school and high school. I still have that inquisitive interest in it.

I never played with make-up or anything of that sort, but even when helping doing the dishes I would combine 2 kinds of dishwashing soap if I had to help get something out that wasn't that easy to wash. It was the same thing with clothes when I didn't want my mother to see I made it dirty or that I fell and had those grass stains all over me. This later continued to interest me because I got acne. So, various kinds of soap, gels, etc. I combined to use both at the same time or made myself a regimen where I determined the amount I would use in the morning and in the evening. And even now while working on making my own line of products I am combining different kinds of shampoos and conditioners. The same goes for skin hidratation. I cannot remember the time where I used only one cream to hydrate my skin and help it regenerate.

These examples may even be a little bit funny to you, but they show the nature you need to nourish in this business. In a more grown-up version of this curiosity you would find out what interests you and your prospective buyers or users and you would find out everything you can about it – how it's manufactured, used, ingredients, what is good, what is bad, what can be improved, etc. You would also show the curiosity about the marketplace around you and internationally, recognizing if the trend is going down, stagnating or rising.

This neatly brings us to the next point. ***You need to be driven and motivated by something.*** This is not a must, but it helps a lot if you're not in it just because you think you like it. Or maybe you even know it. It is more probable that you will get further in your endeavor if you or someone close to you has a certain problem and you WANT to fix it. Nietzsche once said, "He who has a 'why' can bear almost any 'how'".

It is very common that people who have a certain health condition or someone close to them has it, that they become doctors. People who have certain legal issues or have been wronged by law tend to focus on not letting it happen again and become lawyers. And if you have acne or your hair starts to fall out, you may be interested in starting a company that makes an effective product that will fight whatever condition you or someone close to you may have.

Or, let's say it like this – you also need to be a little selfish, you're making the product not only for other people to use, but also for yourself and because you want to use it. I did not want to make my shampoo because I wanted to make it for everyone else. I also made it for myself. I still have hair and I want to have it in the future and instead of eventually losing it, I would rather improve it.

This is the reason why *you also want to make a difference, not only money*. There are a bunch of companies out there who are there for the profit. They will advertise to you that they can help you, but very often those products are very cheap and they tend to make very little difference if any. And call me idealistic, but "How do we make the most money" isn't the idea and core value you want to make your company on. You want it to be profitable, but first things first.

For you to set yourself apart from any company like that you need to want to make a difference. *You need to have a desire to work in this field* and to improve it. Ferdinand Porsche once said, "In the beginning I looked around and, not finding the automobile of my dreams, decided to build it myself." If you do not improve anything in the product you want to sell and only re-package and change the sticker on the box, then you're not doing anything. Eventually, your customers will recognize this and you will be stigmatized for this, especially if there is a company out there with the same product that is better and wider known than yours. Herman Melville once said, "It is better to fail in originality than to succeed in imitation".

Apart from finishing law school (never really was a lawyer) I like to describe myself as a photographer, entrepreneur, author and a serial improver of things. Are you someone who likes to improve things? Adam Grant describes the process that the economist Michael Housman went through like this... There is actually a simple internet browser test to determine this. No, you don't need to visit a page or anything, just answer one simple question: Do you use Chrome/Firefox or Internet Explorer/Safari? The Chrome/Firefox users are the ones who are not taking things for granted, challenge them, improve on them and they stay at a job for 15% longer. How does this simple test tell us this? Well, the answer is simple. For Chrome/Firefox you had to challenge what came preinstalled on your computer and look for something better, make additional effort to find it and install it.[1]

I really do not recommend you use someone else's product and only repackage it, but if you do... At least then make the packaging more appealing or

---

[1] A. Grant, Originals: how non-conformists move the world, Penguin books, 2016., pg. 4.

practical, improve it. If it's a shampoo maybe you can add a hook or a textured, easy to grip surface people could use to get to it easier. You should be representing YOUR company and selling YOUR product, so there has to be something of yours in it. There are many Elvis Presley impersonators, but people only love The King.

Please do not get frustrated that there aren't enough problems you can solve or anything new you could invent and become the next Unabomber. Yes, that's how he started, by being frustrated because he thought that all the world's hard problems were solved and all that was left are the easy and the impossible ones. But many companies have succeeded just by evolving and improving on things. Starbucks didn't invent hot water, they just started using it in a better way. Same happened with Google and search engines and Apple in mp3 players. (Ask Sheldon how he feels for choosing a Zune). Facebook wasn't the first social media website, I believe that my first profile was on hi5, but Facebook is now the leading name in that category.

While I will never advise knocking-off a formula and using it as your own, I must admit that this can be used for good too. Not knocking-off, but analyzing the formula of your prospective competitors or a formula of a product or a company you aspire to, etc. Take it as research of the market. If you are able to do this you will have insight in what a certain company charges for a certain product that has certain ingredients in it.

Creativity is one of the more important things in any business. Children often develop theirs playing games, be it with other children or finding solutions to some problem in a video game. So, from time to time I am not against playing a game if you can squeeze in the time even as an adult. You may think of yourself as someone who is not creative, but it is also a trainable skill. Writers who have writers block will sometimes just start writing random words on the paper, sometimes even gibberish, until they have dealt with their block and they are ready to write on subject again. Sometimes forcing yourself to do something related to what you really want to do is actually training you in that field and inviting ideas.

There are several other ways to enforce creativity and new ideas. One of those is brainstorming. Basically, this is a concept where people get immunity from criticism for giving random ideas from which something good can come out. Not only is the verbal criticism forbidden, also any sign of smiling at someone, raising eyebrows or making any facial expressions which would say that someone doesn't approve are basically banned from brainstorming. There is also reverse brainstorming. Here, instead of trying to get the best idea, the participants actually start from the idea and try to dissect what problems could occur during the implementation of the idea. Similar to brainstorming are focus groups. The difference here is that these can be smaller groups than brainstorming groups and here everyone is chosen for their expertise in their field. While brainstorming groups can have people from various backgrounds, focus groups have people with similar backgrounds. There are, of course, other techniques and you will need to find what suits you best.

There's one more distinction here I want to make. Being creative doesn't have to mean that you are creating something completely new, going from zero to one. You could also go from one to ten. I often say about myself that I am a serial improver of things. Even if I am sometimes not great at creating something nobody has ever seen before, I do see potential in some ideas and how to make them even bigger and better.

You need to be at least somewhat communicative. How do we define this 'somewhat communicative' term? It's fairly easy. You probably wouldn't call me a communicative person if you met me for the first time. I mostly nod, give some signs that I haven't fallen asleep, etc. I am a great listener. And even when a person I was talking to has forgotten about our conversation I tend to surprise by doing something they have never expected to see or hear or receive. Being good at communicating doesn't have to mean that you are this talkative person that doesn't know when to shut up. Being communicative also means following the conversation, listening and asking good follow-up questions.

This is another thing how you as a small business will be different from the bigger company you may be afraid of. You can give value to your customers by listening to them and what they are saying. Include them in the developing process and let them help you create the product you want. Allow them to be as passionate for it as you are.

Which brings us nicely to the other form of being communicative. It is very well known that even a 'quiet person' becomes chatty when sitting behind a keyboard. So, either you or someone you hire or start the company with should be responding to every e-mail you get in a timely fashion. It is very good to make one message that will automatically respond when you receive an e-mail and say that you will get back to that person in 24 or 48 hours. It can be seven days for all I care, as long as you do not ignore the people who are interested in you. The same isn't true when dealing with prospective business partners, business deals, etc. Those you should try to answer in 24 hours, never longer than 48.

Even if you are a really communicative person, do not spend too much of your time writing long e-mails. Sometimes a longer clarification may be needed. If that is concerning one person, then take your time. If that is concerning more than one person and let's assume something happened with your batch of products, then you may want to send an e-mail to everyone in your mailing list or possibly address them in some other way. At least now it's not too hard to publish anything on YouTube and share it on your social media sites.

Being communicative is also a trainable skill. Most of the time there are only two reasons one is not communicative: a person is shy or a person does not think he or she can contribute to the conversation because they do not know something about a certain topic. Shyness you can work on by putting yourself into positions you wouldn't normally be in, going out more, trying new things, etc. Just like people who are catching snakes can develop immunity on a certain venom if they are bitten often enough. Sometimes they even inject themselves with small amounts of poison. Which is to say that you need to consume your "venom" in small doses until you deal with it. Reading books and having at least one new word a day will help you build your vocabulary and be more eloquent when speaking. Also, if you feel like you don't have much to say about yourself, you can always pick up a newspaper (do they print those anymore?) or just read about several different topics on the internet: politics, celebrities, cars, movies/TV shows, health and the current news from your field of work. Always read the breaking news, most of the people will be talking about that. And try to follow stand-up comedy.

Why is this important? Because being communicative will be beneficial to your self development and also to the development of your company. As a more communicative person you will be able to better communicate with your eventual employees, you will be able to represent your company and products better, you will be able to influence people better, you will not be scared when answering an unprepared question.

You need to be focused. Focus is one of the things that is crucial in the world of entrepreneurship and persistence from the next chapter will build on this just fine. *Focus means that you need to **follow one course until you are successful**,* as Robert Kiyosaki said.

Me personally, I do not believe in ADD, it is my opinion that we just have more information at the tip of our fingertips, which is the reason we can lose focus easier. Back in the day when you had to spend hours in the library to find what you needed to know you couldn't afford to have ADD, to lose focus. *The only way you will succeed is if you do not allow your distractions to become your focus.*

You need to divide tasks. The curse of an entrepreneur is the controlling spirit. We always want… need to be included in everything that is happening, so we can be sure everything is going right. But this is very similar to driving. Think of being included in every single task like driving very fast on the highway. When you are driving fast your field of vision narrows down and more and more you only see what is directly in front of you. As soon as you slow down you get a much clearer and broader picture of the whole situation that you would have otherwise missed if you were going faster.

This also allows you to take a step back, take a deep breath and clear your mind for a minute. Again, we as entrepreneurs don't really do well with serenity. But if you can stay in the loop of what is happening and allow yourself to take a long weekend to re-charge your batteries, that will not only be good for you, but also your business. You are no good when you are exhausted and you will make more mistakes then.

Do not be afraid if you have some of the seemingly negative characteristics. Insecurity and similar "negative" traits can be turned positive. Barbara Corcoran once said that "Those who are nervous about failing can become hyper-focused on success". Doubting if something will work may lead you to improving further on it and making an even better product than you already had. So, while at first negative, this may push you to always try to be better. M. L. King almost didn't become the president of the Montgomery Improvement Association. Michelangelo almost didn't paint the Sistine Chapel, because he viewed himself a sculptor, not a painter. He even fled to Florence for two years.

You may be "taking too many risks". But in risks entrepreneurs see potential. We forget that the very definition of the word is *a person starting a business, taking on financial risks in the hopes for profit.* Even so, good entrepreneurs only take *calculated* risks. And not even only calculated. Many of the best entrepreneurs aren't great risk takers. They may take more small risks, but they very rarely make big ones. More often they make small risks that could yield great rewards, covering the downsides of the risk. You may be selfish, but like I said, this could be a good thing. I am also selfish. I want to help others, but I want to help myself too. My products are good because I don't want anything less for myself.

17

1.2 How you need to act

I believe we have covered enough of what needs to drive you and what you need to be like internally to be able to succeed in business. But there is also that external part that you are able to nurture and you will need to nurture if you want everyone else to see you as someone they want to work with.

When Ashton Kutcher was asked what he is looking for in new companies, one of his answers was – extraordinary entrepreneurs. So, what do you need to do to become this extraordinary entrepreneur? 7 things:

1. You need to be strategic
2. You need to be persistent
3. You need to be decisive
4. You need to be open to advice
5. You need to be frugal
6. You need to be transparent
7. You need to be dressed for the job you want

What does it mean when I say *you need to be strategic*? This means that you will need to be able to create various strategies. You will need to have a funding strategy, marketing strategy, selling strategy, etc. But you will also need to be strategic in your communication – when finding partners, presenting ideas, pitching for funding…

Often we get carried away and because we are so passionate about our products we want to tell people everything about it. We love it, why would we not share it with the world? Because you don't have an NDA (Non-Disclosure Agreement) with the world. Most of the time you want to be passionate, but also not give everything. You want to give enough general information and some specific to you, but only enough to hook the deal, not to present someone your idea which they may decide to take for themselves.

Persistence really pays off. Rarely will you get it done the first try, it is important to endure. Your persistence will not only show what type of person and entrepreneur you are, but also how much you care for your product and therefore your customers. The successful man is the one who does not quit the race 3 meters from the goal. Napoleon Hill puts it in another way, talking about a man who has been faced with temporary defeat when his gold vein dried out. This man quit, sold his mining gear and left. The man who bought this gear went to the same spot, consulted an engineer who then told him that what the people before were mining was a fault line and the real vein is only one meter from the fault line. It doesn't matter what kind of challenge you face, is it funding, not finding partners or being rejected by someone – stay persistent. Try again, fail again, fail better.

This also doesn't mean to be pushy or too aggressive. You need to be able to show people you want your dream to happen, not stalk them. Even if you are accepted or someone said they would call you… Be inquisitive, show initiative – you call them or send them an e-mail and see how things are progressing.

You need to be decisive. This means that you are willing and able to deal with some tough choices you will have to make as an entrepreneur. Maybe it's relocation, firing someone or something else. You are the pillar of your company and you need to have a backbone. Many famous successful people have succeeded because they were able to decide on something and stick to their decision, like Henry Ford did when he was told that the engine he envisioned was impossible to make. That being said, you don't need to show the backbone by being rude to your employees, people you work with. And I hope you never mistake decisive for stubborn. It has many similarities, which is why you need to be really careful, but the main distinction is that a decisive person is not afraid to admit that someone else may be right.

Being decisive is a very much needed skill because you will not always be presented with an opportunity, they come and go. You will be called upon to take it or leave it. Or as Eminem put it, "If you had one shot, one opportunity to seize everything you ever wanted, would you capture it or let it slip?"

Decisiveness is also one of the signs of confidence and confidence will also be positive for you and your work. Jordan Peterson says how you need to stand up straight with your shoulders back. This advice isn't only physical, it is also psychic, metaphysical. This means that you accept the burden of your work, your obligations and, ultimately, of your life, your Being… decisively. "People, including yourself, will start to assume that you are competent and able (or at least they will not immediately conclude the reverse). Emboldened by the positive responses you are now receiving, you will begin to be less anxious. You will then find it easier to pay attention to the subtle social clues that people exchange when they are communicating. Your conversations will flow better, with fewer awkward pauses. This will make you more likely to meet people, interact with them, and impress them."[2]

But even though you need to be decisive, you also ***need to be open for advice***. You need to know that you will not always know everything, you will not always have the best ideas and you will not always be right. Admitting to yourself and people around you that you do not know something is a strength and don't be afraid to show it.

OK, maybe you don't really ***need to be frugal***, but you certainly don't want to throw the money around that your investors gave you, whoever they are. You should be conducting business and using that money as if it were your own. Be careful what you are spending it on and if that is really needed or a luxury. I am all for luxury, I love it, but when starting a company, having it open is a luxury. Once you are standing on your own feet and are able to keep paying back the investors and paying your employees, then grant yourself whatever you can afford. But still keep in mind that the company needs to keep making money and don't bring it to its knees.

Unless you are a character from a comic book, you can't really ***be transparent***, but when working together with partners and investors they should be receiving regular updates of how the company is doing and any news about some developments and changes – minor changes, you can let them know by the end of the month or a quarter; major changes, you let them know IMMEDIATELY.

It would also be beneficial to you and your company if you had ***leadership skills*** and people around you perceived you as a leader, even if, possibly, you aren't one yet. It isn't easy being a leader and it's even harder thinking of yourself as a leader if you have doubts about your expertise and if you aren't perfect at everything. As an entrepreneur you will certainly come across some things you do not feel comfortable with and which will be new to you. We usually only feel comfortable as leaders if we know everything about the problem we are facing, which isn't always the case. And the times when we don't know everything about everything shake our confidence as leaders. "Leaders are always risking making fools of themselves. The willingness to risk how they look is one of the things that makes them leaders."[3]

---

[2] J. B. Peterson, 12 rules for life, an antidote to chaos, Penguin random house, 2018
[3] M. E., Gerber, E-Myth Mastery, Collins Business, 2006, p. 72

Leadership skills are many and they range from business to personal skills and emotional intelligence. I won't go into all that. I'll just remind you of communication once more. A leader is also great in communicating what he wants and needs to be done by his employees, by his manufacturers and doesn't leave much room for interpretation. "In the mind of the entrepreneur, the business is already done before he starts it. In the mind of the enterprise leader, the objective then is clear, even if the process isn't."[4] But his greatest communication skill is listening.

Finally, you need to *dress for the job you want, not the job you have*. And here we will interpret 'dress' a little bit wider than only clothes. We will say 'dress' in the way that you will also put on your best behaviour and best skills, social and otherwise. You need to dress, behave, invest in yourself and visit social events for what role you want, not the one you currently occupy. People will often tell you not to judge a book by its cover, but that is exactly what the cover is for, otherwise all covers would be blank with only the title on it.

1.3 Are habits good for you

What is a habit? Other than being something a nun would wear, habit is also a recurring behaviour you have taught yourself to do. It is basically the muscle memory of psychology. And while many people would say that it is bad when your love life becomes a habit, it's rarely the case when you are an entrepreneur.

Many successful entrepreneurs have some habits and/or rituals they follow. Some are useful, some are quirky. But the ones we would focus on here are the ones they consider have improved their life and productivity.

In reading books and articles and watching interviews many entrepreneurs mention some kind of *meditation*. Not everyone is using the same technique or anything, but they are doing it. Some do it in the morning and the evening, some only once a day, they use different applications for it, etc. So this way they are trying to keep fit mentally, which is very important in today's day and age and it is very good that people have started talking about this, breaking some taboos. And in today's world where we are almost addicted to stress and the fast lifestyle it is good to have a part of the day when you can just sit and calm down.

---

[4] Ibid., p. 117

Speaking of sitting and calming down... Some of the people who are interested in trying meditation aren't actually sure what they should be doing. How do you sit? Where do you place your hands? You don't need to do any Yoga positions to meditate, do whatever is most relaxing to you. You don't need to cross your legs, you can just sit on a chair, close your eyes and imagine your goals. You can even sound them out and give the meditation another dimension. Chase Jarvis describes his meditation like reading the article in the newspaper.

Meditation can be just a few moments of clearing your head from all the distractions and imagining something you wish to accomplish. Maybe your meditation is a prayer. Every person will adapt this to themselves the way it suits them best.

Many people, but mostly men, tend to have issues with meditation at the start because they see it as too soft or not masculine enough for whatever reason. Eventually those people turn around, but until you do if you are a more physical person you could try a martial art I fell in love with a while ago, which is Aikido. It is a softer martial art, it basically has no attacks, other than for purposes of training to defend yourself, you can find schools that focus a lot on breathing too, etc. It is important to do your research on these, since there can be some schools that are overselling this, but as a martial art, a philosophy, even a way to live and move through the streets, Aikido is very good.

Apart from keeping fit mentally, you should also try to **keep fit physically**. *Mens sana in corpore sano*. Which would translate to 'healthy spirit in a healthy body'. I do not say you should now be an Olympian, but your brain and muscles do communicate, so you should start jogging, going to the gym, working out in a park, whatever you like to do to keep fit. One research even proved that people have become more productive while they were doing their job standing up instead of sitting down.

A major one is ***planning and scheduling***. Many entrepreneurs have admitted to have been avoiding this because they felt constrained because they didn't want these limitations, they didn't want to be told what they need to do. But the truth is, you make your calendar, not the other way around. And when they did finally adopt this practice suddenly they started claiming more time for themselves. Because they did schedule and they didn't have this hectic lifestyle and work ethic, now they could schedule time for meditation, time for the gym, time just to walk with their family. Elon Musk apparently schedules his day in five-minute blocks. Now, this may be too OCD for you, but it may be a habit you should try. What is not too OCD is having a time of day when you check your mail. By checking and answering your mail only two times a day you will train yourself and your colleagues that this is the time when they can expect you to answer, but you then also free your time during the day and you don't put on these electronic handcuffs on yourself by trying to respond to e-mail immediately.

Scheduling doesn't only mean that you are dedicating time for some activity, but also that you are reserving time for yourself. Many entrepreneurs we very often look up to, Mark Cuban is one of them, will agree on one thing... The most precious thing you have, that you cannot control or buy, is time. When people reach this epiphany they usually change how they spend their free time and stop paying the same amount of attention to TV shows, computer games, etc. and make the best use of the only time they have to spend with their loved ones, investing more in themselves, see the world... We only have a limited amount of hours on this earth and it is our job to use our lives to the best of our abilities and make every grain of sand that falls in this sand clock count.

So while it is a great thing to have a plan of things you are going to do, you can even take it one step further. Make a plan of what you are not going to do. So, you made a schedule when you're responding to e-mail and taking calls. Make a decision to not do any of those outside of that time. Make a decision to eat healthier, walk a certain distance every day, take a cold shower for 1 minute... Whatever you wish and whatever you think will help you.

Every one of us is sometimes guilty of *procrastinating*. I am not going to suggest you somehow stop doing that, since it's more or less inevitable that you will do it. To whichever extent. But you will need to make a choice what you will be procrastinating on. This will make a difference between you being a high or low performer. I am also procrastinating on something, but I am doing it while writing this book, so I'm really hoping it turns out to be good. Brian Tracy calls this creative procrastination. "Creative procrastination is one of the most effective of all personal performance techniques. It can change your life."[5] The key to this kind of procrastination is to not let procrastination take you over without you noticing it, but that you procrastinate on purpose.

Adam Grant calls these procrastinators the originals. These are the people who are a little bit late to the party, the sweet spot procrastinators. They are not early and they are not doing what they need at the last moment. Leonardo da Vinci

---

[5] B. Tracy, Eat that frog!, Hodder & Stoughton, 2016., p. 33

has painted the Mona Lisa from 1503-1506., only to continue working on it until 1517. By not planning everything out and by not putting a "finished" sign on your work, whatever it may be, you are leaving yourself open to ideas, for improvement. Procrastination can be bad when speaking about productivity, but it can be good when speaking about creativity.

Speaking of Musk, he and many others are *early risers*. If you don't have enough hours in your day, get up an hour earlier and see what you will be able to do with that extra time. That extra hour for your business could catapult your productivity and income. Musk also goes to bed late, he has admitted in several interviews that he sleeps only 5 hours a day. Admittedly, many other entrepreneurs are now reflecting how they have been boasting and bragging about how little they sleep and now healthy sleep is crucial for them.

Entrepreneurs will also tell you how you need to work hard and the riches will come. Which isn't a lie, but it also isn't the only truth. While, you do need to work, you can also *work smarter, not harder* and achieve the same goal. Bill Gates also once said that he would rather hire a lazy person to do a hard job because the lazy person will find an easy way to deal with it.

It is a recurring statement that the entrepreneurs and various successful people like to read. Self-development is a very big and very important investment. This will also go back to keeping your mind fit, but the reason you want to do this is to *keep perfecting yourself*. "Upgrading your skills is one of the most important personal principles of all. Learn what you need to learn so that you can do your work in an excellent fashion."[6] If you are expecting people to follow you, you need to be the authority in your field and have good work behind you. Try to focus on something too. We will talk about this later, but you do need to narrow down and can't really dabble in everything.

How do you become the authority? By doing what you want to be. As Austin Kleon says, too many people focus on the noun, not the verb. They want to be a writer, but don't write, want to be a photographer, painter, singer, but don't photograph, paint or sing. You can't be the noun without the verb. Also, many people who are just starting out are impatient. Not even a month goes by and they are feeling down because they do not have 100,000 or 1,000,000 subscribers so that they can just earn from YouTube. Books like this one and the ones I am suggesting are for people who are willing to walk the mile, not for the ones who

---

[6] Ibid., p. 63

want to earn by playing games and making fun of themselves on YouTube. YouTube is a great platform, but there is a lot of trash and you need to distinguish the signal from the noise and find yourself a role model and an aspiration outside of playing games. I do not condemn games, they are also a nice tool for developing creativity, but I cannot take it seriously if that is the peak of your ambition.

Keep track of your business. Keeping track will train your discipline, but what is even more important is that it will give you a baseline for your growth. How do you scale a business if you do not know what it is at now? How do you improve anything if you didn't take the time to measure it? You can't. If you want more sales, then you need to know how much you have now so that when you do get more you also know by how much this period grew.

Keeping track of your business and everything else that is going on will also help you to make use of the *Pareto principle*, also known as the *80/20 rule*. Broadly speaking, this principle states that 80% of your effects come from 20% of the causes. You could also interpret this that 80% of your results come from 20% of your efforts or that 80% of what you earn in the company comes from 20% of what you do there. Which is to say that, if you are selling products, 80% of your sales come from 20% of your customers, so instead of you catering to the whole 100% of your customers you could possibly do that only for 20% and make the same amount of money, if not more for providing them with a better service and dedicating more time to those 20% customers.

And don't be mistaken, this is a principle you can apply to anything. Vilfredo Pareto lived from 1848 to 1923. He was an engineer by training and was managing coal mines. Later he succeeded Leon Walras as the chair of political economy at the University of Lausanne in Switzerland. But how did this principle came to be? Pareto first noticed that 80% of the peas from his garden are produced from 20% pea pods. Later, he also noticed that 80% of Italy's land was owned by 20% of its population. Microsoft found out that 80% of the crashes are caused by 20% of the bugs. So, you see, this principle isn't even evolving, you are only witnessing, sometimes unknowingly, the constant discovery where it can be applied.

There is even a thought that we may find too simplistic, but it can be effective. And that is that you can *make your bed* before you go and try to change the world. Even though it is small, by doing this in the morning you are actually starting a day with one task already accomplished. Accomplishing this first task of the day can attract more positive outcomes. Bed can become a room, a room can become a flat and a flat can become a world. If, by chance, this doesn't happen, you will always have a made bed waiting for you as something positive, stimulating and encouraging and it will provide you with needed rest for the next day.

This being said, please be advised that these are not a recipe for success. This is an example of some good practices, but you may need to find what is a good habit for you. Copying a habit won't put you in someone's shoes, but it may put you in that mindset and you may discover you have more time and are being more productive. But while trying out these habits the best thing you can do for yourself is realize when you are at your productive best. Keep a log, make a productivity map and track for a period of time how certain behaviour affects your productivity. Other than the habits, you should also track places. Maybe you are most productive in a certain room, in a park or somewhere else.

1.4 Motivation

This may not be your personal attribute, but you may want to read, listen or watch other peoples failure and success stories. One book I will recommend you read is "Think and grow rich" by Napoleon Hill. I may not recommend many other self-help-like books, but this one may be valuable not just in your business life, but in general. Just like some do with "Art of war", business people quote and love this book.

Sometimes when you read or listen to someone's story you may be disheartened, you may consider it more of an anti-motivation, than motivation. But the troubles some of those people have had show you that it is worth going forward and fighting through those. Often when we see people who have accumulated a great wealth we only admire their triumph, but we rarely recognize the amount of defeat they went through before getting there. This is the side effect of the social media and people being presented with only the best moments in a life of a person or a company, but the reality is very different. The problem is that nobody is bragging on Instagram about how they failed. And they maybe even should. Imagine if you documented your way and had a little documentary about your journey. You could be the inspiration for many others.

Of course, today it's general knowledge to know about Bill Gates and Steve Jobs starting from a garage, etc., but before I have started this endeavour I have read the book mentioned above and I have seen a lot of interviews of Elon Musk. These interviews have scared the hell out of me. Elon Musk mentions one of his friends who says starting a business is like chewing glass and staring into an abyss. Elon has lost a lot of money at several points in his endeavours, maybe even gone bankrupt. But he was a visionary. He was one of the PayPal owners and he eventually sold it. From that money he funded his next company, then he moved from that one to another, coming to Space X. At space X he has come to a point where the launches were failing or weren't successful enough. He had money for three launches and all three weren't a success. Even then he somehow found the money for a fourth one and was given a short deadline when we're talking about space programme. The fourth one was a success and now he is planning to go to Mars.

He is behind the idea of a great looking electric sports car which is also autonomous. In the "regular" car industry there isn't very much improvement. Yet if you look at Tesla it looks like all the improvement has been put into one car. Even though the cars may not be the greatest, I admire the company for this innovation. His two marriages have failed and there has been a lot of problems on his way to greatness. But he had a vision and was convinced it was worth doing it. Be convinced it is worth doing what you are doing.

One of my favourite quotes by Musk is: "I am not trying to be anyone's saviour. I am only trying to think about the future and not be sad".

Having said this I must add that I wouldn't really advise spending too much time on this and not enough time on your actual business and your work. Why? Because it is easy to lose your way while admiring these people from the distance. You begin some retrospective of how good and successful they are and where you're at, etc. Basically, you're comparing your journey to someone else's highlight reel. People show you only the Steve Jobs and Elon Musks when they built a great electric vehicle and a rocket. We may all enjoy rooting for Elon Musk to further push the advancement of electric vehicles, space travel, to be successful with the Boring company, etc., but it is very hard to relate to people like Musk, Warren Buffet and the other icons of the business world. So the reason why it would be advised to stop googling these people and reading about them at a certain point is because you want to cut down on your insecurities and self-doubt at least until you do that first step and start your own journey. I made a motivational song playlist on my YouTube so I can listen to it while working, resting, whenever I need it. If it helps you, look it up, but YouTube is full of similar lists and you could always make the one that suits you best.

1.5 Have role models

It doesn't really need to be from the same industry. You can have Elon Musk for your role model if you like because you may like his personality, endurance, perseverance, values he stands for, always improving and innovating, etc. Actually, I hope that you will have role models from other industries as well, because that will be the sign that you are able to filter out what you don't need and only take the useful stuff (steal like an artist[7]).

But you shouldn't only have people as role models. You should have some companies you look up to (and past). It is good to have one to five companies you... don't really have to look up to, because you may want to go past them and make your products even better, but it will give you a better reference as to where you would like to be and what you would like your products to be like.

When I was starting out I have listed up to five companies I have considered good. Then I listed which products I would like to make and then listed examples of those products. And I have had examples from more than those five companies, but those five have left some kind of an impression on me that I wanted to be reminded of every time I work on my ideas.

---

[7] The title of Austin Kleon's book.

2 Defying the rules

Artists are very much like entrepreneurs and entrepreneurs are very much like artists, all need to hustle to get good at the game they are playing, increasing their skill and their sales. But these are not the only things that artists and entrepreneurs get good at over time, they also get good in breaking some of the rules.

Now, since I do have a background in photography, I'll try to use it as an example to explain this as best as I can. Many photographers when they have no idea what they are doing and when you would refer them to a rule or a set of rules would, unwilling to learn, respond with „But rules are meant to be broken". And this may very well be true. But you also need to know what rules you are breaking and why you are breaking them in order to break them to your benefit. If you are breaking the rules only because you do not know them or are not able to follow them and perform at that level, then you are not breaking them effectively. It is in this efficient breaking of rules where creativity is born. „Learn the rules like a pro, so you can break them like an artist", as Picasso would say.

2.1 Do you need to be an expert

Some people will tell you that you need to be an expert in your field. You don't. People claiming this aren't 100% wrong, but they aren't right either. Guy Kawasaki said that the experts are clueless. It was the experts who said that Facebook and YouTube and other products that have gone beyond success would fail. "Lance Armstrong is embarrassing the tour", said the Head of the Tour de France on Lance's return in 2009. "Coldplay is the most insufferable band of the decade", said the New York Times' Jon Pareles. "We don't like their sound, and guitar music is on the way out", said Decca Recording Company, rejecting the Beatles in 1962. "The grotesque scribblings of a child have a naiveté, a sincerity which make one smile, but the excesses of this school sicken or disgust", said Emile Cardon on Monet, Renoir and the other Impressionists.[8]

Did you know that J.K. Rowling hated her job as an administrative assistant? Did you know she quit her job and started writing Harry Potter books? Did you know that she couldn't find a book deal at first? Did you know that

---

[8] The quotes are taken from Chris Guillebeau's book The Art of non-conformity.

Madonna was fired from Dunkin Donuts or that Walt Disney was fired from a publication he worked for or that Robert Redford was fired from an oil company?

Yes, you will need to have some knowledge of what you are dealing with. This knowledge you will need to be able to better present your ideas, your project, your company and your product. However, as a smart and strategic entrepreneur you will become, you will also know that you cannot do everything by yourself and you do not need to carry the collective knowledge of your company. If you are dealing with cosmetics, you can't be the chemist, the person working in production, retail, marketing, etc. How good you are will become evident with how many good and smart people you gather around you.

A clear example of this is a person probably everyone knows about and that is Henry Ford. When Ford was told by his engineers that it is impossible to create the engine he wanted, he has envisioned, he told them one thing – produce it anyway. Henry Ford is a success because he understood and applied principles of success, one of which is desire. This is only one proof that the expertise can often be a handicap, because smart people are often very good at making simple things complicated. Not to say that Ford wasn't smart. Being intelligent has nothing to do with having a diploma, it's just to say that an uncluttered view and a mind free of learned boundaries are the ones that challenge and change the world. "Forget the experience curve. The most powerful force in business today is the inexperience curve. Young companies, born on the right side of the digital divide, are running circles around their older, richer, and slower rivals. If one wants his or her company to think outside the box, why not learn by working with people who don't know there is a box?"[9]

Actually, in the movie Head of State Chris Rock gives a closing speech where he addresses being called an amateur. This is what followed: "You're right, Vice President Lewis. I am an amateur. When it comes to creating so many enemies that we need billions of dollars to protect ourselves, I'm an amateur. When it comes to paying farmers not to grow food while people in this country starve every day, I'm an amateur. When it comes to creating a drug policy that makes crack and heroin cheaper than asthma and AIDS medicine, I'm an amateur. But there's nothing wrong with being an amateur. The people that started the Underground Railroad were amateurs. Martin Luther King was an amateur. Have you ever been

---

[9] It's a Great Time to Be an Entrepreneur, http://bnoopy.typepad.com/bnoopy/2005/06/its_a_great_tim.html, quoted in Marc J. Dollinger, Entrepreneurship: strategies and resources, fourth edition, Marsh Publications LLC, 2008., p. 4

to Amateur Night at the Apollo? Some of the world's best talent was there: James Brown, Luther Vandross, Rockwell, The Crown Heights Affair, The Fat Boys, Rob Base. But you wouldn't know nothing about that. Why? Because when it comes to judging talent and potential you, my friend, are an amateur!"[10] *(Somehow I feel like I need to say that this is a quote about being an amateur, not endorsing any policy.)*

An educated or, in this case, an expert person is not always the one with the greatest amount of knowledge. An educated person is also the one who knows when, how and from whom he can acquire anything. "Any man is educated who knows where to get knowledge when he needs it and how to organize that knowledge into definite plans of action."[11] The man who can organize and direct a group of experts to accomplish his goals is as much of an expert as the group he is directing. "If you can learn to identify (and then use) other people's expertise, you'll build momentum so much faster than if you try to learn everything yourself. Curiosity is very powerful, but no one can know everything, and the sooner you accept that, the better. You have to learn to identify and ask for the help you need, because you must be able to delegate the tasks you don't like to do or are not especially good at. You will never succeed at the highest level as an entrepreneur if you don't focus on doing the things that are your Unique Ability®, to use a phrase from the world's top coach for entrepreneurs, Dan Sullivan."[12]

In order to prove to the world and to Henry Ford himself that Ford was "an ignorant pacifist" a lawyer asked him a plethora of general knowledge questions. When Ford grew tired of these questions in response to a very offensive one he replied: "'If I should really want to answer the foolish question you have just asked, or any of the other questions you have been asking me, let me remind you that I have a row of electric push-buttons on my desk and by pushing the right button I can summon to my aid men who can answer any question I desire to ask concerning the business to which I am devoting most of my effort. Now, will you kindly tell me why I should clutter up my mind with general knowledge for the purpose of being able to answer questions, when I have men around me who can supply any knowledge I require?'"[13].

Just like Henry Ford, Andrew Carnegie also personally admitted to Napoleon Hill that he knew very little about making steel, but he surrounded

---

[10] Chris Rock as Mays Gilliam in Head of State, 2003.
[11] N. Hill, Think and grow rich, Quarto Publishing Group USA Inc., 2015., p. 70
[12] B. Kurtz, Overdeliver, Hay House, 2019.
[13] N. Hill, Think and grow rich, Quarto Publishing Group USA Inc., 2015., p. 69

himself with people who could do everything he couldn't. This is not dissimilar to Niccolo Machiavelli's *"Regent"* (Il Principe) where he speaks about a ruler surrounding himself with good advisors.

It is great to have a background in something and have a degree, but sometimes to me it feels like it can be a crutch and that you can do more if you don't. "The official story is that I completed a two-year master's degree in International Studies at the University of Washington. The real story is that I spent $32,000 to learn about motivation", said Chris Guillebeau in his book *"The art of non-conformity"*. Don't get me wrong. I'm not saying education is not important and you should leave school or college. If for nothing else, education is great for maturing and figuring out what you like, learning to learn and being social.

I have now written a book about starting a cosmetics business, about landslides and about photography. Which only shows how far the interest in a specific field and your dedication will take you. And the fresh, uncorrupted pair of eyes is always good. In this book I say I'm not your cosmetic chemist or your makeup artist and I am not a geologist either. I love to be a researcher. Every time something interests me I can go online and find something out about it. Or buy and read several books, like I did while writing this one. Why is this good for me? Yes, there is a lot of noise on the internet and you need to recognize the signal, yes there is a lot of trash. But this then starts working out your ability to critical thinking and when you do that now you can challenge some things based on what you know and what you have read and found out, now you can state those things in a different way and you can simplify them. There are people out there that do not challenge what is delivered to them. Any news, any information, any conspiracy theory, they eat it up. This is why I believe that my books are not only good, but very informative and close to the person it was written for.

Notice, I've gone from writing about landslides to cosmetic entrepreneurship. It's not even remotely related. Why I am better at this than some of the people who are more established in these fields is because I do not have these professional deformations where I would be using some heavy university-level language that the people you are essentially writing this for cannot understand. People who have issues with landslides do not need definitions and names of a certain part of the body of the landslide. And let's face it, more often than not, those are not the people who have the education for that. At least in the region where it was written for. Very similar to cosmetics, why would you need some complicated knowledge about formulations when you can take care of the part of the equation that will help you be different and appeal to customers. It's not bad to have that knowledge so you know when a laboratory is messing with you, but it's essentially not needed for this business. Especially since we're going to cover the laboratory part to get you as ready as we can.

2.2 A laboratory

Unless you are making natural cosmetics you will not be able to make cosmetics from home. And even if you are, you will need some equipment before you start "cooking". For making cosmetics at home you will need to fulfil the FDA manufacture procedure and you will need to follow up on other regulations such as labelling, FTC regulations, etc. Not to say that laboratories only mix chemicals, they don't. You can make natural cosmetics in a laboratory as well, but with more precision, consistency in the ingredients used and speed.

You can have all of the above, but you do not have a laboratory and have no idea how to find one. I was in the same situation. I have first done all the research, even learned more about the growing market before I found the laboratory I wanted to work with.

You will need to figure out what you want from a laboratory. Some will only work with female cosmetics and only create hair colours. Some will work exclusively with certain ingredients, etc. You could even use a laboratory as a marketing tool. A certain type of consumer will place great value in cosmetics which are made in Italy or France instead of cosmetics from Poland. USA residents often place value on products that are made in the USA. If this is something you want to use as a quality stamp then you can get more information with the FTC (Federal Trade Commission). European residents will value if the product is made in the EU. Some countries also cultivate their precise and quality work, so you could see stamps like 'German quality' or on watches 'Swiss made'.

So, once you have decided what message you want to send, now you can go and type in 'laboratories in…' in a search engine and open several. You need to know that not everyone will reply, but sometimes the ones that do will be that much greater.

As you can see, finding a laboratory isn't hard, but it isn't that easy either. Finding a laboratory or even 10 on the internet is the easier part of the search. But once you have found it and after you have filtered out those who are not making the cosmetics you want to create, now you need to contact the right person in the organisation or write to a general info@... e-mail and ask them to pass your inquiry along. If possible, use your e-mail client for two reasons: 1 – so you can be sure your e-mail was sent and 2 – you will have a list of who you have already sent an e-mail to. Use the contact form on their website only as a last resort. After that, the laboratory needs to answer and if they answer, they also need to be available.

I mentioned following up earlier. This is how I decided what laboratory I wanted to use even if it wasn't in France or Italy. I received a response to my e-mail and even before I had a chance to read it the CEO who answered the e-mail followed it up with a phone call. This dedication to a prospective client you know nothing about or what amount of money he could bring you was what made me want to work with them. And I did have replies from Italy, France, Switzerland and Norway.

Who knew this would be a place to quote science fiction, but let's do it anyway. Peter Capaldi as Doctor Who said: "Human progress isn't measured by industry. It's measured by the value you place on a life. An unimportant life. A life without privilege. The boy who died on the river, that boy's value is your value. That's what defines an age. That's what defines a species."[14] This is how you decide who to work with and this is how people will decide to work with you – give value and reward when value is given to you.

Once you have been fortunate enough to find such laboratory, you will need to talk shop. This means that you will need to tell them what you want your products to be and some of this information may be what will become your signature. This is why you will need to get an NDA (non-disclosure agreement) between you and the laboratory. After that agreement you will need to agree on who owns the formula. This will not be possible with private labeling because you are only re-packaging a product that you did not develop, but if you are not doing that then you should make sure that you are the owner of the formula. The formula usually comes in a PIF (Product Information File) and laboratories usually try to keep it. I am not sure if it's required for them for some sort of inspections or they just want to make sure you stay with them. In case you have to change a laboratory for any number of reasons you do not want to go through R&D again, so this is also important if you're serious about your business. R&D cost for some more complicated products can go up to 3,000 USD, while they can also be much lower for simpler formulas. Some tests are included in the price, some additional ones

---

[14] Doctor Who, Thin ice, season 10 episode 3, 29.04.2017.

you may need to pay extra. So you see why you would rather want to skip this part, apart of it taking time.

After you get the agreements done laboratories will usually provide you with a letter you will need to fill for each product you want to make. This letter will contain information like: what ingredients you want in your products, what you don't want, colour, scent, should it be vegan, target market, what attributes you may require from your products, how much you wish to charge for your product (target cost), how long it should last for (shelf life), type of containers, type of closures and more.

Feel free to reference other products. Maybe you even want to send a sample of it. While I was deciding on what I want to make I spent a lot of money on ordering different kinds of products. At the time of writing this I have over 10 hair styling products around me. Some I used only once, some I still do.

After all of this has been done, you have signed the NDA, you have sent your letter about all the products and you have paid for the R&D, now you wait. Research and development phase is something that takes usually several weeks. After those go by, the laboratory will reach out to you and send you the samples to be approved. Some laboratories have the maximum number of times they will be reworking the formula and sending you samples, so it's good to know that beforehand.

You will need to do some testing on your products. Some general testing is usually included in the price, while for some more specific testing you must pay more. *Stability testing* will show you if your product will remain stable during its lifetime on the shelf. Typically, this is one to three years. Acceptable pH, viscosity, colour, scent, appearance and functionality are some of those tests. You could also do *package functionality testing*. This test will possibly include closure clog testing, leaking testing, drop testing, etc. Since many products are water based they require some sort of preservatives to ensure they do not become contaminated by anything. This will be tested with a *microbiological test*. *Safety testing* is not required by the FDA (Food and Drug Administration), but you basically want to spend a little bit more money, so you can avoid eventual liability claims. And I want to encourage you to contact the FDA anyway or refer to their website as the regulations may change or you may have a certain type of product. All the products we make come in touch with the consumer in one way or another and it should be tested if this product is safe for use. Contrary to popular belief, testing on animals in this stage is not a must and certain types of tests can be done artificially or test on humans. Before ordering a large batch you should probably do some *consumer testing* too. You have most likely by now tried your product on your skin or hair, but there are other skin and hair types out there and you may get some very helpful feedback that you didn't think of before. *Claims testing* is something you will need if you want to use the efficacy of your product in marketing or say that it removes dandruff in X amount of days or reduces the lines around your eyes by X%. The fact that some of the other companies do not do this properly, doesn't mean that you should do the same too. "Only 18% of all claims made in commercials for cosmetics are generally trustworthy. Cosmetics firms often use advertising verbiage like "clinically proven" or "inspired by groundbreaking DNA research." But researchers combed through these claims and found that the majority were vague and many are outright lies, according to a new study published in the Journal of Global Fashion Marketing."[15] And it is not a bad idea to have your products dermatologically tested as well.

Sometimes the laboratory that is producing your product will also be able to offer you some kind of packaging. We will divide the packaging into two different categories: primary and secondary packaging. Primary packaging would be the *container* that holds your product and the type of *closure* you are using for that container. Secondary packaging is any packaging that will surround your finished product. There is also labelling of the packaging. And the corrugate or the box that is used to ship multiple units of your products. When talking about secondary packaging it isn't bad to see how your prospects feel about ecology. Some companies won't have secondary packaging in some countries and in some they will, all because people in some countries are so into the environment that they boycott products with secondary packaging. For example, they will not buy toothpaste if it has a cardboard box.

It is advised that you have your packaging done even before the point of going into production, so you could also test how the containers will react to your product and vice versa. When choosing a packaging there are some hidden costs you may want to consider. Packaging companies will have some moulds already done and ready to be distributed. These are the usual moulds they make and they will not be unique to you. However, there is usually an option of changing colour or something similar. If you want to go with something more unique, then the price will also be a little bit more unique. The company will need to make a mould only for you and you will be charged as such. This is no small matter, because if I am

---

[15] A. Siferlin, That Makeup Ad Is Probably Lying to You, Time Health, http://time.com/3973031/cosmetic-ads/ [Accessed: 26.11.2017.]

not too wrong this price can go even up to 50,000 USD, which is why people usually go with changing the colours instead of the shape.

Up to this point you were still working on a relatively smaller scale. Now what you will be doing, or what the laboratory will be doing for you, is a scale up. This means they will take the formula they have made for the smaller amount and scale „the recipe" up to be suited for larger amounts of products.

After this, you will be at the production and ordering phase. When ordering how much of a certain product you want different laboratories work with different minimum numbers. Some laboratory may say they will do a minimum of 250 units, while others have a weight minimum (e.g. 10 kg). You will also need to determine your own minimum amount with the money you have to pay for everything and the amount of product you expect to sell in a year.

If you expect to sell a certain ammount of product in a year, let's say it's 8.000 units, it would be best to divide that into quarterly orders. You want to rather have 2.000 units on your hands and sell those and then reorder instead of sitting on 8.000 units that have a certain shelf life.

Keep in mind that you will have to order the next batch of products on time and not when the last one goes out. The laboratory may need to get the components for your products and suppliers of those have something that is called *lead time*. Lead time is the amount of time the supplier takes to process the order and possibly make the components and ship to the desired destination.

2.3 Establishing a niche

What does it mean when people tell you that you should establish a niche? That means that you should research the market and narrow down your focus. What they are basically saying is that when starting out you can't really start with men's cosmetics, women's cosmetics, baby products, consulting, marketing, photography, etc. So, to determine this you ask yourself a few questions. Does the market leader have any weak spots? Maybe he is only comited to only selling a certain way. So you offer additional ways to sell your products, maybe directly from you. Maybe the market leader hit gold and now he stopped innovating. Which makes you stronger because you innovate. Find the questions you can ask for your business.

While doing my own research I have seen that quite a few companies actually have products that they add that 'for men' sign and they consider it done. But from the top of my head I can only remember one that has an anti-shine powder, good for TV presenters for example.

Very often when giving advice to people who are starting a new business in cosmetics and are thinking of starting their own line people say you should establish your niche and start with one product. And that is the safer way to do it in regards to you investing a smaller amount of money. „Always err on the side of starting too small. The reason is simple: it's easier to dominate a small market than a large one. If you think your initial market might be too big, it almost certainly is."[16]

However, this does not have to be the safer way of doing business and creating your brand and image. Maybe your product isn't only one product. Maybe your product is a set of products. In order to have a complete product or a complete offer you envisioned maybe you want to have a shampoo, a shower gel, a face wash and hand soap as a package. Maybe having all of these quality products will be your signature. Maybe you can't send your message of a healthy clean life without those.

Why are you establishing a niche? Well, the basic idea is that you would like to be the first in something. „It's the law of leadership: It's better to be first than it is to be better."[17] And I don't want to say you shouldn't establish a niche, but sometimes you just ask yourself, „what for"? It's not like there are certain areas that have no products at all. Some companies when they couldn't be the first in a category, they would create a category for themselves. Until a few years ago I would laugh if someone told me they were a pet photographer. Not someone's pet photographer, a photographer of pets. People have built studios around this concept. But what if you can't be the first? Not being the first doesn't need to be that horrible. The first movers who create the market had a failure rate of 47%, while the improvers only had the rate of 8%. So, you can't be the first in the marketplace, we established that it is not such a bad thing, but that shouldn't prevent you to try and be the first your prospective clients would think of. „It's better to be the first in the prospect's mind than first in the marketplace."[18]

---

[16] P. Thiel, Zero to One, notes on startups, or how to build the future, Penguin Random House, 2014., p. 53

[17] A. Ries, J. Trout, The 22 immutable laws of marketing, HarperCollins Publishers, 1993., p. 3

[18] Ibid., p. 15

You also shouldn't be overextending yourself. Many companies have noticed a drop in their sales after creating another product. Doesn't matter if it's something with 'light' after the regular name or something else. The people who were buying your product may swap and now buy the 'light' version, but you are not taking any new customers from another company. This doesn't mean that you should have only one shade of lipstick, but if you are creating shampoos, it does mean that you shouldn't have too many of those.

So, yes, establish a niche, but don't allow anyone directing you away from the direction you feel connected to and passionate about.

2.4 Don't fall into the trap of 'Passion'

Sometimes the worst advice that someone could give you is that you should go and pursue your passion, do what you are passionate about. This advice comes from various places, sometimes it's parents, life coaches, partners, friends… Hopefully we can assume that these people do not want anything bad for you, so while they are most likely saying this out of good intentions, they may make things worse.

But it's better to focus on the things you spend most of your time on. I'm not suggesting you start earning money playing Nintendo Wii, but it is much better to invest in something you are dedicated to, instead of something you are passionate about. Even the wording is different… dedicated TO and passionate ABOUT. 'About' is more distanced. You could be passionate about basketball, but you are 150 cm tall and the most you do is shout advice through the television to the professional athletes. This does not mean that you would be dunking over Shaquille O'Neal.

To put it in another way... Passion is a very strong emotion that drives you and which you cannot always control. Hate and love are very passionate emotions, this is why you will hear that someone has committed a crime of passion because of a strong and sudden impulse and feeling.

It is good when the thing you are dedicated to and passion come together, you will not feel like you are working a day in your life and we rarely quit things we are good at and which we enjoy. „Entrepreneurs should know that the most successful business ideas succeed when their passion is in tune with their skills and when the idea represents a business opportunity."[19] But passion is just a generic answer people tell you when they don't have any other advice and a more important one is the dedication and what you feel as a calling and your calling will likely be passion + dedication.

Do you even know what your passion is? If you haven't tried enough things to discover this, you may not have a clue. Even Napoleon Hill went and did several jobs, lifted several companies, magazines, etc. and left those to his partners, most of the time without any payment. Only later he found that what he enjoys is teaching people how to become better at sales, but also at business and life in general.

2.5 Speech

Just like the title suggests, this one isn't that much about defying the rules, but it is about defying some of the "rules" of speech. And that means not using some of the common phrases that we usually find harmless, but they might be registered by others as dishonest, deceptive or, in general, not give the best picture of yourself.

As a business person you will need to communicate well with other people, pitching your product and company to others, forming partnerships, dealing with other companies, negotiating, etc. You will need to lose the 'I mean', 'like', 'erm' and similar words you use to fill in the pauses you make when speaking. Practice speaking like Obama. That can't be bad, right? Speak slower and make short breaks as if you were thinking and avoid those words like that. You will also need to avoid some other phrases that we find harmless, but aren't.

- *'As soon as possible' or, even worse, 'ASAP'*. You do not want to use this because when working with business people they tend to have schedules and calendars. ASAP doesn't mean anything. They don't know what soon is, when it will be possible. If the job needs to be done, do it or give them a time frame, don't set yourself up for procrastinating for a month.
- *'To tell you the truth' or 'truth be told' or 'in all honesty'*. So, what have you been doing up to now? Not telling the truth? Avoid this also. You may think I'm overthinking it, but even if the conscious mind doesn't register this, the unconscious one might.
- *Stop starting or ending sentences with 'Believe me' or 'Trust me'*.

---

[19] Bruce R. Barringer, R. Duane Ireland, Entrepreneurship, Successfully launching new ventures, Prentice Hall, third edition, p. 11

- *Stop asking people 'you know what I mean', 'you follow me', etc.*
- *'As far as I know'* may be your attempt to answer something honestly, but I said it before, there is nothing bad in not knowing something. I admire people who say that they do not know something. They will ask someone who does or look it up. Do not give inaccurate information to appear smart or for any other reason for that matter. Or as Jordan B. Peterson would say, be precise in your speech.
- *'To the best of my recollection'* is just a euphemism for 'I don't know, but I think that…' Don't guess if someone is asking you for information and relying on you to give accurate answers.
- *Repeating the question you were just asked or saying something like 'that is a good question'* can be a sign of stalling for time. Avoid the usage of these.

I may be grasping at straws here trying to make it informative and interesting for you, but if you take away one thing from this part, I hope it's this. Never use the phrase 'as soon as possible' or 'ASAP'. This I learned while helping in a disaster relief in Bosnia and Herzegovina, working with people from an organization called SOS Attitude. This wasn't just a name for them. They really had the SOS Attitude and there never was any stalling when going somewhere or providing help. Apply this to your business and everyone will be happier – people you work with, people you work for and even you yourself.

But when we address the speech, there is actually more to it than just using our words. A very large part of our communication is actually non-verbal. So, in order to be the best at communication, it is rarely enough to just have the words memorised, you also need to show that you mean what you say and that what you are saying is true. I can't go into too much detail about this in this book, but I highly suggest you read some books on body language, even the ones that cover criminology, maybe even take a course.

3 What is good to have for a good business

To operate a business you will need to have something registered. Now, you could start something that is called sole proprietorship, but it is rarely advised. It's easier to open and close, but in this type of entity you are responsible with your own assets to anything that may happen with your products. Whereas, if you create an LLC – Limited Liability Company – only your company and only its assets are in danger should something go wrong.

3.1 Starting a business

Before we go any further into this, maybe it would be beneficial to first see who is actually starting a business. So, who starts a business? Sometimes it's just someone who wants to help others and has a solution for some of their problems. Other times it is someone who is unemployed. But often it is someone who wants to escape the yoke of his boss because that someone feels like he is doing everything around there anyway. This person Michael Gerber calls a Technician.

A Technician is a cook in someone else's restaurant, for instance. Accountant in someone else's accounting firm, salesperson in someone else's car dealership, a lawyer in someone else's law firm, etc. These are all the people who do their very best and their boss is "just yelling orders". Suddenly there comes a thought in their mind and they come to the conclusion that they are "carrying this company, doing all the work around here and that they could do this better by themselves without someone breathing down their neck". This Michael calls an Entrepreneurial Seizure. Suddenly, a Technician is turning Entrepreneur.

And there is nothing worse than a technician turned business owner. Why is this often the truth? Because many technicians fail to learn, refuse to learn, anything about running a business. They do not know what is going on, but they see that they are too stretched out. Maybe eventually they realize that you can not be effective even in what you excel at as a technician if you have to also be the entrepreneur, manager, cleaner and your own errand boy. "In fact, rather than being their greatest single asset, knowing the technical work of their business becomes their greatest single liability."[20] While being a technician there is so much that doesn't get done in the role of an entrepreneur and manager.

---

[20] M. E. Gerber, The E Myth Revisited – Why most small businesses don't work and what to do about it, HarperCollins Publishers, 1995., p. 13

If anything, I would say that it would be easier for an entrepreneur to do the other two roles than any other way around. Because of the spirit and the nature of overcoming challenges of the entrepreneur. I am not saying this would be great and a right thing to do, not only because he would be overstretched, but because the entrepreneur might not enjoy the work that a technician does and customers could feel that in their experience with the company.

You will also find out that being an entrepreneur is a little bit more important than being a technician. "There is nothing wrong with being a Technician. There is only something wrong with being a technician who also owns a business! Because as a Technician-turned-business-owner, your focus is upside down. You see the world from the bottom up, rather than from the top down."[21] I say that it is a little bit more important to be an entrepreneur than to be a technician because if you are not an entrepreneur then you are only trading jobs. This time around you have even more responsibilities you need to deal with. And when starting a company you are not starting a job, you are starting a business. Once you realize that and that your purpose is now in creating jobs for others you become an entrepreneur. And at least for a short while you then become a manager. Because once you start creating those jobs you will need to do that. People will be looking up to you, your employees will need direction and leadership, not just support by doing the job of a technician together with them.

When a technician finally gets his first employee, usually a person to do the books, his newfound freedom suddenly allows him to be more creative. And not just in the product or service, but running the business too. When finding your new employees and delegating work, you will need to be careful how much of the control you will give up in certain aspects. Give up too little of the work and you won't have space for your creativity, give up too much and in time you might get faced with unsatisfied customers or work that you would have done better.

But what does this technician need to do to actually get there and start his own business? Well, let's look at that for a moment too.

---

[21] M. E. Gerber, The E Myth Revisited – Why most small businesses don't work and what to do about it, HarperCollins Publishers, 1995., p. 38

3.2 Business plan research

For a good business it is good to have a decent business plan. When dealing with anything you should try to remember the old British Army adage, known also as the 7 P's: Proper prior planning prevents piss poor performance. If you are planning to ask a bank or someone similar for money to help you start this business then you will even need a great one.

In this plan you will research your potential market. You will address who your potential customers are. You will need to do some other things too, but even more importantly, you will predict what challenges you may run into during the process of starting up your business.

You will need to research the names when considering *what name you want to use* for your company and product as it may be Trademarked - ™. This is also something that will cost you money, but you will protect yourself and your product a little bit better. When thinking of a name, you should be careful about choosing a name. When creating a company you always need to know what you are going to be doing. You do not want to have a cosmetics company called Downtown Bakery. "When you are choosing a brand name for your website, the first thing to ask yourself is, what's the generic name for the category? Then that's the one name you don't want to use for your site."[22]

The names of your business and the website can differ a little bit, but you still need to have certain "conditions" met. You will want the name to be short and/or be able to shorten it even more. Some examples of this are Coca-Cola, shortened to Cola or Coke; Carl-Zeiss, shortened to Zeiss. Carl Zeiss actually dropped 'Carl' from the name not too long ago. "People feel closer to a brand when they are able to use the brand's nickname instead of its full name."[23] The name should also be simple and use as few letters as possible, Coca-Cola is using 4 different letters to form an 8 letter word. Are you more likely to remember the name like Datsun or Nissan?

You can try to be unique and suggest a category with the name, but that is becoming harder by the day. You want a speakable name. If you want to use the word of mouth, you should take into consideration that there are people out there who are dyslexic and that number isn't small either. It is also good if you can think

---

[22] A. Ries, L. Ries, The 22 immutable laws of branding, CollinsBusiness, 2002, p. 150
[23] Ibid., p. 154

of a name that has a verb potential. This is explained more in the marketing part of the book about owning a word.

You will also need to *determine what is your brand*. A brand isn't only your name, logo, colours… A brand is also your message, feeling people get when they hear about you, etc. A brand personality. What does your brand communicate to your buyers and how? What values does it stand for? What problem does it solve? Determine what makes you unique in the marketplace, what do you have that nobody else does? And most importantly, create your brand before you create your product. It will be much easier to promote and launch your sales if you let people know about you beforehand and not when everything is ready to go.

Don't be mistaken, you will need to answer these questions and more to build a good brand. You may think that you are limiting yourself. Well, you are. And you should. Only when you limit yourself do you have a brand. You can't be everything for everyone in every situation. You can't solve problems of the whole world. Your brand has to stand for something. That is why the limitations you may be scared of are essential for your brand. These limitations and consistency are what is going to build your brand. Rome wasn't built in a day, either. But it burned in one.

You may be living in a smaller town where you can't really hope to sell a lot of your products, so you will need to take this into consideration. There has also been some research that *the culture and environment* where people live will influence how much of the product people are using, but this is more tied to men and some parts of the world still feeling too macho to say they use anything.

So, where will you be selling? If you are from the USA or want to sell there, then you may need to get the FDA approval. If you are from Europe or want to sell there then you will need to consider those regulations. If you want to sell your products in Europe, you have to follow the cosmetic Regulation CE 1223/09 (which came into force on July 11th 2013) according to which the persons responsible marketing the products under their own trademark must submit some information about the products they place or make available on the European market (Article 13) through the Cosmetic Product Notification Portal (CPNP), the new online notification system. The new cosmetic Regulation CE 1223/09 also requires that each product has a PIF (Product Information File) containing all the information established and required by the national and community regulations in force. The great thing is, wherever you're from this is something most laboratories will do for you. The not so great thing is, most laboratories are very attached to the

PIF or PIP (Product Information Package) as this also contains your formula. If you are interested in all of the legislation for EU, you can check that here[24].

Addressing your potential clients will also be a challenge. You need to identify who is using your products. Of course, you may want to say that you want everyone to use your products and that is fine. But what you are doing here is not excluding people, it's just focusing your limited resources on reaching people who are more likely to buy. Remember the Pareto principle? 20% of your customers make for 80% of the sales. If you're working with female cosmetics, your age range may be from 7 to 77, so you will need to narrow it down to your focus group. If you are working with products for men, the age range is somewhat smaller and it varies more. Men start using hair products sooner than skin products. It may happen that in the teenage years they start using hair styling and face wash more, maybe a scrub also and, of course, everyone is using shampoo. Only later will men start using something like a hydrating cream, eye cream and some other care.

Identifying your main target group can help you determine your brand personality too. Is it going to be made for businessmen – elegant, classy, serious. Is it going to be made for a younger audience – sporty, playful, funny. But here is another twist. Some men still do not buy their own cosmetics, but get something bought by their girlfriends. Rarely wives, they wouldn't want you to get better looking and find someone else. But joking aside, who are your customers really? Are those men or their other halves?

By determining *demographics* you will determine the sex, age, income, geographic area, education level, marital status, occupation. Sometimes people will claim that certain product is for a certain ethnic group too.

How do you get this information? You could try doing it on your own, but I do not know if that is a smart idea. Not because you do not know what you are doing, but because you may not be as objective as a professional market research firm. But since you are most likely just starting out, let's assume that money is limited and you need to do it on your own. How would you do it? Internet. You have 90% of information at your fingertips. There are also some specialized business and government institutions that could have the information you need. Census Bureau, Bureau of Labor Statistics, Small Business Administration, Chamber of Commerce, Department of Commerce are some of the "tools" you could use. You could also have your customer fill out a questionnaire when they

---

[24] https://ec.europa.eu/growth/sectors/cosmetics/legislation_en

visit your store or you could make a pop-up window asking them to do that when leaving your website. And if you're selling on your website, you should already have enough customers to make your own statistic and see who comprises the majority of your customers. You should know who and how many new ones are there, who are the old and returning ones, who spent how much, etc. You will, most likely, be able to find out who your best customers are and that will give you a head start in working smarter and not harder. Knowing your best customers will enable you to use the virtual velvet rope and applying the 80/20 rule start catering more to the 20% and possibly earn even more than trying to please all 100%.

You could also delve into *psychographic* elements and determine attitude, personality, value, hobbies, lifestyle, etc. Or, in other words, answer the question 'why they buy'.

The psychographics should tell you the mental state of your customer when he is making a decision to buy a product. The customer will suddenly get the sense of purchase motivation. He or she may find it out through your marketing or by getting to a certain birthday and showing more interest in their looks. For example, collagen production reduces after the age of 30, so this could also be a purchase motivator. People may buy your product because they are not content with how they look. They buy because you are reinforcing the message that your product will help them alleviate their problems and indirectly raise their self-esteem. They may have been this experimental customer, who has now returned because of the functionality of your product and because of its performance, so they are now grateful and place higher value in you and your product and perceive it as "worth the money".

You may think that your product is the most important thing you have and once you have it you are done. ***You must also have a good business design***. You do not want to have to think about money every time you go to bed, you want to have a business that will work for you, that will be creating money for you automatically, that will be sustainable.

3.3 How does a business plan look like

Well, there is more than one answer to this question and it usually starts with asking what you need it for. To give you a summarized definition we could say that a business plan is a formal statement of your business goals, reasons you think they are attainable and ways to attain them. If it's a business plan for a bank or something similar then it will take you a lot of time to write one. It will be at least 25 pages of presenting your company, name, idea, vision, marketing, who is your target audience, how will you reach them, etc. And it can go up to even 50 pages.

Bernhard Schroeder, the Director of Programs at the Lavin Entrepreneurship Centre at San Diego State University, has the following elements of a business plan: executive summary, company description and mission, products or services, marketplace and competitive analysis, strategy and implementation, organization and management team, financial plan and projection.

If you have worked for or with any NGO and wrote a project proposal, this is it. A business plan is a pumped-up project proposal for getting the investors to trust you and invest in you. Here you will be showing off your knowledge of the industry, the market, users, customer, etc. But every business plan and every project proposal start with a good and concise summary of what is going to be presented. That is your *executive summary*. This is sometimes all that the people reviewing your project proposal or your business plan read. Make it great. *The company description* should say more about the company, who you are, how you came to be, what are your goals and your mission and how do you plan to achieve those. The company description should not be confused with the company introduction, which will feature things like the name, type of the company, who runs it etc. The goals should be SMART, which means that they are **s**pecific, **m**easurable, **a**chievable, **r**ealistic and **t**ime bound. *Products or services* is just what it says, you will describe what goods you will be leveraging to become profitable. *Marketplace and competitive analysis* is where you'll most likely shine. Knowledge in this field will set you far apart from others who did not do their homework. Find out the trends in your industry, how fast is it growing, by how much, who is your competition and why, why isn't someone else your competition, what are you bringing to the table to set you apart and how will you compete. *Strategy and implementation* is the way you are going to approach the marketplace. *Organization and management team* will describe your company's structure, who are the owners, partners, etc. *Financial plan and projections* is something you should consult a professional person on, but it will need to plan for your liquidity, how much you will be spending where, how much you plan to earn, etc. Lawyer and an accountant are probably going to be one of the more important roles you will want to have in your company or at least to have someone consulting for you.

Every business plan should also have a title page and a table of contents. The title page is a separate page with the title of your business plan, date and your name and address. Table of contents appears after the summary and before the body of the plan.

While your business plan will be a compilation of knowledge of the whole team, it should be written only by one person. Some people are better at translating their thoughts on paper, or, rather, screen. You do not have one person writing the plan just because someone is more inclined to writing, but because someone will be reading the plan and you want it to be uniform, using the same language, instead of people reviewing the plan seeing the stitches in it. If you need help writing a business plan, there are also some computer programs dedicated only for that – one of those is Business Plan Pro[25]. It costs around 100 USD, so if you can afford it, try it out. It contains over 500 sample plans, free books and is generally easy to use.

You can also familiarize yourself with a 4P model by E. Jerome McCarthy from 1960s. The 4P's stands for Product, Price, Place and Promotion. Which means you first need to determine your *product*, which, if you got this far, you probably already have. You will need to know the number of your products and their specifications. You will also need to know how you can sell your product. While selling you will, if that is possible, need to measure how many first purchases you have and how many are return customers. Return customers are the ones giving you sustainability. The second P is the *price* of the product. You will need to know this beforehand to give it to the laboratory too. Because you do not want to have production cost above your price. This can't happen, of course, but still. You need to include your product, packaging, profit margin. When all of that comes together you have the price of your product. *Place* is where you determine where you will be selling your product. Without getting too much into detail here, any direct sales you can do without including large store chains or something similar will yield you more profit. But still, if you're doing it on your website, you'll have those expenses. *Promoting* your product has become much easier with the internet and social media.

And you will need to answer all of these questions and more. For a bank and most serious investors who would like to see their money back to give you anything you need to present them with a good plan, show them that it is possible and that what you are presenting is realistic and not idealistic. Of course, a good and practiced pitch and charisma can be a great bonus, because if you can charm them, then you will be able to take that skill to the negotiating tables.

---

[25] https://www.businessplanpro.com

But if you're making a business plan for yourself, then it can be approached a little bit differently. I still advise researching the field. I know I am repeating myself, but this is how important it is. So, you will find out about the field, you will find out about your audience, you will at least have a general idea about some things like sales, marketing, etc. You need to know which ingredients you want to use and which ones you do not. You should have someone you look up to, which company you would want to be like or maybe even better. What are you aspiring to? You will need to know what is setting you apart, you will want to research if there is a possibility to have partners who can help you in your endeavours and you will determine what your key activities will be in your new business.

Now, I don't want to go into detail on this, but there is a simple tool you can use. You can check *the business model canvas* on the internet and you can find a cheat sheet on Google on how to fill it if it needs more explaining. You can see the canvas below.

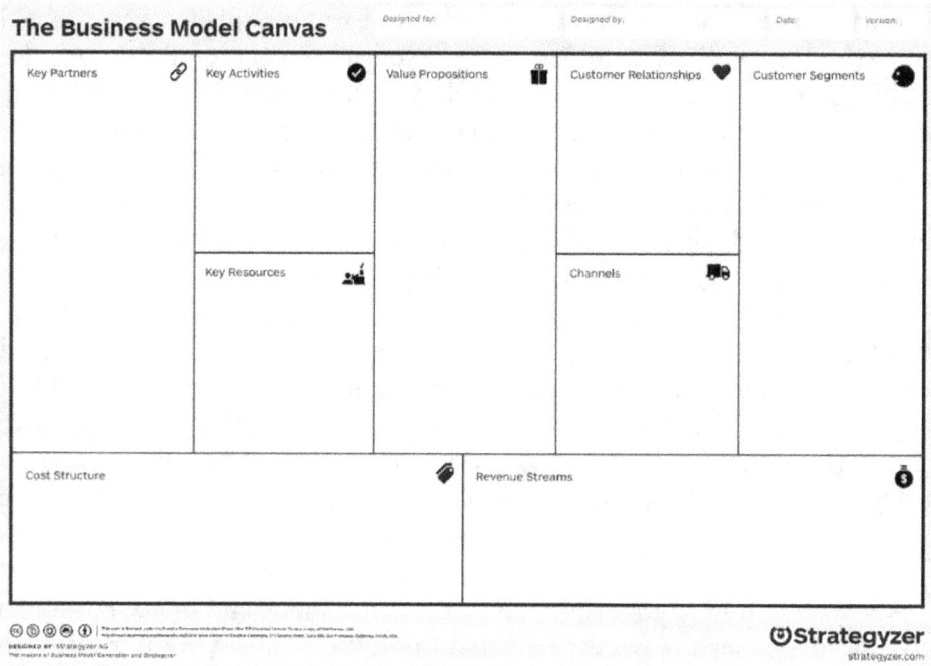

Picture 1 The Business Model Canvas, used with pemission of Strategyzer.com

But this all being said… This is what you need to consider, evaluate, you don't want to go in blind into anything. But never and I mean **NEVER** allow a business plan to pull you back. Do NOT wait for it to be perfect, because it never will be. We are our own worst critics and if it were up to us we would never finish a book, a poem, a painting. Like the great DaVinci once said, „Art is never finished, only abandoned". You will NEED to abandon your business plan and start making it a business reality eventually.

As you start making your business plan a reality you will find out why it didn't need to be perfect. Because you can come across something you did not expect and that can start a whole domino effect. You may have determined your consumers wrong and you may attract a different age group, you will need to address them differently if they are significantly younger or older, etc. Whatever the reason, you will encounter some things on your way that will make you do things differently than you have planned. This and the fact that the market and many more factors are changing faster today than they did before is the reason that even Tony Robbins says that it is much better to have a business map, not a business plan. A business map means that you are not predicting anything, but that you understand the teritory and because of that are able to adapt and adjust when needed.

But I still want to stress the fact that you need to learn about the field you are interested in, about the market and everything you can. Even if the business plan ends up not being useful as a business model, it was still useful in nurturing your idea into your conciousness, it was the thought you woke up with and went to bed with. I am not a big believer in the power of the mind, but I do think you should convince yourself how good this is and that you will make this happen. And even knowing I may sound like a fortune cookie you need to remember that you are your own biggest enemy. **„The reasonable man adapts himself to the world. The unreasonable one persists in trying to adapt the world to himself. Therefore all progress depends on the unreasonable man." – George Bernard Shaw.** Please, be unreasonable.

3.4 Predicting the challenges you may face

Entrepreneurs do not have problems, they face challenges and they overcome them. Predicting the challenges you may run into is probably the most important part of the plan. I have ran into people who think that this is being negative and may put a barrier in your mind and slow you down, but I disagree. I disagree because you don't need to see that as a barrier, you can look at it as a milestone you need to achieve and evaluate yourself there.

You will have much more success and it will be much easier to evaluate yourself and check what you are doing wrong and fix it if your milestones are smaller – you need to make a difference between a milestone and the goal you are trying to achieve. Thinking of the challenge you are predicting as a milestone will give you the motivation to get there and past that instead of fearing failure because of it.

Sometimes it is even more important to define your fears. Give them voice. Maybe you fear that your start-up won't be a success. So what is the worst thing that could happen? You stay at your current job. Usually, when you define that fear and the worst thing that could happen, it suddenly isn't that horrible anymore. Yes, it would be bad if your start-up doesn't launch, but as long as you learn from it, you did not fail. So, the worst thing that could happen to you is... What? You work for a boss a little longer and eventually start a new project or get some more money together before you try again, refine the idea, research a bit more.

While doing this you will also need to do something that is called a SWOT analysis. SWOT means you need to determine what are your **S**trengths, **W**eaknesses, **O**pportunities and **T**hreats. You will be making this yourself, so it is imperative that you are honest to yourself, there are no upsides to lying to yourself and making up strengths you don't have. The more honest you are, the better you can address the challenges you encounter. **„A problem well stated is a problem half solved" – Charles Kettering.**

3.5 The vision for your company and product

We spoke a little about the vision before and wanting to improve something. You will need to figure out what is your vision of your company and your product because this is what you will later use in your marketing. In the business world there is a saying „going from zero to one". One may seem like a small number and a small step, but that is the largest one, zero to one represents innovation. Something that nobody else has. Going from one to whichever number means that you are improving something that already exists.

What are you going to offer that is different? Will you offer an improved product? How is it improved? Is it a special ingredient that is added? What did you add and why? What does the ingredient do to the product? Did you remove something that was bad in the product? Why was it bad? Did your product go through some special tests and does it have some special certificates or awards? Is it cruelty-free? Is it vegan? Is it paraben free, sulfate free? Is it made in USA or EU? Is it...?

But not only in marketing. Your vision, your guiding principle, your mission statement is what you will fall back to when you get to an obstacle or when you need to decide the next step for your company. If your vision is to make skin care safer, then you will have a statement that will remind you of it at all times. When you come across an ingredient that you can't decide should you use it or not, you can fall back to this statement and ask yourself is it safe for people? If yes, then it's one thumb up. Maybe you want it safe for animals too... Two thumbs up. Get enough answers and see if they align with your statement. If they do, you can proceed.

3.6 Marketing

If we were to break down what marketing is, we would find out that not many people know that. So, let's just try to make a difference between some of these names people use as synonyms for it. If you were to put up a sign of some kind or do a commercial, that is *advertising*. If you were to put up a sign on a car or something else and then drive it through the town, then that is *promotion*. Let's imagine the Red Bull car for a moment. If the Red Bull car crashes because the driver fell asleep, then that is *publicity* (and irony). If you get the people involved to laugh about it, then that is *public relations*. If the people start buying the product now, that is *sales*. And if you planned the whole thing, that is *marketing*.[26]

Once you have a successful startup you may have a good deal of publicity around you and your company and products. You need to be aware that this will die out sooner or later and that you will need to shift your focus from publicity to advertising. There was a saying that only two things were certain: death and taxes. Add advertising. One more thing you should know at this point is that it isn't important who you know, but who knows you.

Many people mistakenly think that when marketing a product the product will do all of the work, because it is better. We focus on facts over feelings because facts are easier to quantify and use in the battle of products. We think that objectivity and the truth would somehow give us the upper hand. It won't. We are not really fighting against the product, we are fighting against the feeling it gives

---

[26] Inspired by The 1-Page Marketing Plan: Get New Customers, Make More Money, And Stand Out From The Crowd by Allan Dib

when a customer buys it. This is why before you even start marketing you should finish branding your product and the feelings people have when they hear about it.

A product will do a lot of the work if it is good, but it needs to be paired with good marketing strategy too. And same goes vice versa. For a marketing strategy to work, the product should be good too. Or as Ryan Holiday put it, „Advertising can add fuel to a fire, but rarely is it sufficient to start one".

Also, don't do marketing to yourself. You are marketing to yourself when you catch yourself saying something like "I like this because…", "I would buy it because…". You know what you are doing and making, you know what you and your product and brand stand for and its quality, you have a full picture. It is now on you to provide your customer with the same picture and very often what you think is enough to convert you, is not enough to convert someone who has yet to hear about you.

Many people, probably 100% of anyone you would ask, think they are making a better pizza, hamburger, chicken than… Take any food that has a chain linked to it. But they do not sell better than those or don't sell at all, they only cook for themselves. Some don't want to, some don't know how. If you want to keep it "in the industry", then you might be making the best soap, face wash, lipstick… But for some reason it doesn't sell at all. And often it is a matter of marketing and not the quality of the product.

You will need to consider what will your marketing be and how you will deliver it. You will not have enough money for an expensive advert right away. Besides, you do not want to spend too much money on a big advertisement agency too soon. Think of the big agency as a leap, but you may walk a greater distance if you do several smaller, but smarter steps. And anyway, you will jump further if you have a run-up. So you need to make a good use of internet and all the social media. Marketers plan to increase their use of videos (75%), visuals (73%), blogging (65%), live video (61%), and podcasting (26%). Ben Horowitz, a venture capitalist, said it very well: „There is no silver bullet… No, we're going to have to use a lot of lead bullets".

Do not think of marketing like something that needs to be set up for the next five or ten years. Yes, a company needs to have certain plans, but those are not marketing plans. A company needs to have its financials set up so it can keep its doors open. As far as marketing goes, it needs to be very flexible. Because no matter how good you are, you can not predict the future and, most of all, you can not predict the competition. Either the one that may appear after you or the reaction of your competitors to your products.

Even while working on your business plan you can start building up your social media profiles and there are a lot of those. You may not want to use the name you are considering just yet, just to protect it a little bit more, but you can use something neutral, but very close to what your product will be.

Do not think of marketing in a strict sense, like an advert on a TV or some dentist endorsing you, whatever you may be doing. Marketing is every effort you put into raising awareness of your company and your products. Some college professor may disagree, but I will divide it only in two categories: internet marketing and classic marketing.

Whichever form of marketing you end up using, you will need to ensure that you speak the language. What does this mean? This means that if you're a tech guy or a science guy or anything that may have phrases that someone who isn't in your field might not understand, you will need to simplify them and translate to a common language. This is why I said that the brochure I wrote on landslides may be closer to the people who needed it than the ones written by professionals in the field. As one theoretician said, "A legislator needs to think like a philosopher, but write like a peasant". Same goes for a marketer. And please try to remember that how smart you are isn't measured in how many people do not understand what you are saying, but quite the opposite. If you are not able to simplify the message in order to pass the knowledge on, then you didn't master it in the first place.

As a marketer you need to make it your mission to not talk *at* the people, but *to* the people. Do you remember the chapter about passion? Passionate about and dedicated to. Same thing here. Talking at the people you are just throwing information their way, not caring what they say or think, not reading their expression, mood, reactions... Talking to the people is quite the opposite and you are talking to their problems and offering them solutions for their specific issue, not some memorized text you need to recite and go on. Or as David Ogilvy put it, "The client is not a moron, he is your wife."

3.6.1 Internet marketing

Today there are so many ways to get next to free marketing, which will mostly cost you your time and you will have only some expenses, but nowhere near an advert making process. In fact, there is a saying that marketing of the future will be like sex, only losers will pay for it. And the future is now.

You can make a Facebook profile. Or if you do not mind using your private one, especially if you have a lot of friends you want to share your product with, then with your current profile you can create a Facebook page. The downside here is if you do not set the notifications and they keep flooding your personal profile. Even if you open a new profile, the page is actually a must. This will allow you to create events, add albums, share how your business is advancing, etc. But most of all, Facebook gives you an opportunity to buy very cheap advertising where you can even select the demographic you want to include. This is also great because the paid traffic (obviously, the one you paid for) will bring you some organic traffic (the free one) just because the friends of the persons who have liked your post etc. will see it too. In 2019. Facebook announced that groups are the future and one of the new features is linking groups with pages.

Facebook is now the main platform for both B2B (business to business) and B2C (business to consumer) marketing – B2B at 43%, ahead of LinkedIn and B2C at 72%[27]. In 2019 Facebook is still leading LinkedIn in B2B comunication – Facebook having 49% and LinkedIn 30%, while B2C went down to 69% after it was on 75% in 2018 and LinkedIn is holding only 4%[28]. The drop that Facebook faced is the first in five years after continuous growth. Social Media Examiner research showed that 10% of marketers will decrease their marketing on Facebook, while 51% intend to increase it, which is a 11 point drop from 62% in 2018.

There are several kinds of promotions you can do here. You usually do not want to promote your page. You also usually do not want to promote the views of your post. What you want to achieve is the engagement with your post and that is the boost you want to go for. This is because you do not want pure views or clicks without engagement. People engaging with your content will be the best way of promoting it and giving it social value. This way Facebook will recognize it and rank you higher when it thinks about showing you to their users. Facebook's

---

[27] M. A. Stelzner, 2017 Social media marketing industry report – How marketers are using social media to grow their businesses, https://www.socialmediaexaminer.com/report/?utm_source=Newsletter&utm_medium=NewsletterIssue&utm_campaign=New

[28] M. A. Stelzner, 2019 Social media marketing industry report – How marketers are using social media to grow their businesses, p. 16 https://www.socialmediaexaminer.com/report/?utm_source=Newsletter&utm_medium=NewsletterIssue&utm_campaign=New

current algorithm likes when posts engage a public to leave longer comments and ranks them higher than 2-3 word ones. Facebook assumes that you have a better connection with the public if you made someone spend more time writing their comment.

The great thing is that Facebook offers you tools similar to the ones you have in your e-mail clients. When someone sends your page a message, you can set it to automatically respond and say 'Thank you for contacting us' or 'We're away for the weekend, convention' or something else. The adverts you place are measurable and Facebook is visited by 1.2 billion people daily. You will be able to see which people you have reached, which have responded the best to your adverts and from which devices. This will help you better determine your audience and see which is the most effective way of reaching them. Speaking of visits, it is useful to know that teenagers, your prospect buyers, according to Pew Research Centre[29] are using Facebook a lot less. In 2017 71% of teenagers were using Facebook and in 2018 that number dropped to 51%, which is a 20 point drop.

This may actually be even a little bit too obvious. What isn't is that you need to be careful how you present yourself and your company and products. So, you will want a nice profile picture for your page, you may even want a profile picture for your personal profile which will let people know about your company and products and you will want a nice cover photo. Also, something not too obvious is that you want to share interesting posts and you don't want to share too many. Make sure that you also have posts which are not asking your followers to buy something, but engaging and connecting with them. Not every post needs to sell something, but it needs to achieve something. Give some value before you ask for something in return. Not everyone is as passionate about your products as you are and you could lose people if you are flooding them with posts, especially if you are selling to them all the time. You will also want to have your page filled out and, if possible, don't leave anything blank. Add some milestones to your company. Never share the same content on multiple websites or social media. Actually, let me rephrase that… Same message – yes, same content – no. You need to change the explanation to the link you are sharing, change the picture that you are adding to it… all these are different platforms and you need to approach them differently. If you use the same message, same image, same everything, people will just think you linked 50 accounts together and you're just spam sharing what you published

---

[29] M. Anderson, J. J. Jiang, Teens, Social Media & Technology 2018, Pew Research Centre, 31.05.2018., https://www.pewinternet.org/2018/05/31/teens-social-media-technology-2018/ [Accessed: 29.07.2019.]

on your website. Facebook is a platform that will let you use even a full chapter from some book, this you can't do on Twitter. On some other platform you may need to write something on a picture. You adapt to the native micro content of the platform, like some photographs that went through various filters on Instagram.

Do **NOT** use *chatbots* for marketing. If you want to set-up your Facebook page to answer that you will respond soon because you do not want that long response time to be on your page, that's OK. But I cannot tell you how many pages I have blocked and reported for spamming. Some of those people I even liked. All because this senseless spamming even when you don't write to their page and they still spam you and try to sell you something. If you have a small bot to say "we'll be in touch" or ask "how can we be of service", then that is fine, but if you come across any page that is aggressive and spammy, even if I do it sometime later, then, please, I urge you, report the damn page.

Only 14% of marketers is using these bots, 32% of those will use them more and 13% will use them the same as before. Over 50% are not planning to use them.[30]

Twitter is another social media site that you may want to include in your business. It does not have all the features of Facebook, but you do not want to afford to not be present on it. Just a few regular updates of what is happening, a photo here or there will keep your profile alive and your audience included and interested.

Having a healthy amount of tweets on your profile will also give away a picture of an active company. Not all the tweets need to be your own, sometimes it can be a tweet from another company that isn't your rival, a famous person or just something someone has said that you agree with, but other people couldn't find offensive. This and interacting with people will actually give a more human feel to your social media profiles. Twitter also makes better use of hashtags and a tweet can reach more people than a Facebook status. Make use of the popular hashtags, but use them with care. I have seen hashtags about genocide or domestic violence used to post some videos someone really thought should be seen.

---

[30] M. A. Stelzner, 2019 Social media marketing industry report – How marketers are using social media to grow their businesses, p. 23 https://www.socialmediaexaminer.com/report/?utm_source=Newsletter&utm_medium=NewsletterIssue&utm_campaign=New

Some of the hashtags you want to be on the lookout for are the daily hashtags. These are the most reliable ones and they may give you more exposure. Some of these are: #MondayMotivation, #MusicMonday, #TransformationTuesday, #TuesdayThoughts, #TipTuesday, #TravelTuesday, #GoodNewsTues, #WednesdayWisdom, #ThursdayToughts, #FlashbackFriday, #FollowFriday, #TGIF, #SaturdayNight, #SelfieSunday.

When sharing your articles on Twitter, or any social media for that matter, it is very convenient to have a plug-in that automatically shares these as soon as you publish them on your website. There is one issue with this approach, though. The issue is that people may recognize your social media profiles just as tools to try and get some traffic, but you'll actually achieve an opposite effect. Especially on a platform that is made to look like a live chat.

Speaking about social media in general, you should sometimes engage in conversations that aren't about you or your product at all. Gary Vaynerchuk gives an example[31] of a person having a conversation with Green Mountain Coffee where they just commented that they liked a song and found it motivational. Sometimes it is more important to connect with people, rather than to advertise to them. You're still doing some marketing, no worries.

LinkedIn is basically Facebook for business people and businesses. You may not accomplish a lot of marketing there compared to some other places, but it's good to have a presence, especially since some e-mail providers now can recognize your e-mail and show your LinkedIn profile. Here people will not learn too much about your products unless you create a page for your business, but you can present yourself as a professional in your field. And once you have started this and done your research, eventually worked together with a laboratory, you will know more than the average consumer does.

Google+ is still an enigma. When I first wrote this book it still existed, so I will leave it here just as a warning. I guess Google+ made an attempt to compete with Twitter and Facebook. I don't know if anyone is using this, but still… Google is always working on its products and having a profile there may or may not influence your „*searchability*" on the internet. With Google phones and possible other Google products in the future this platform may take off and you could be one of the first to recognize it and use it to your benefit. On the other hand, Google has spread to so many things and therefore is really quick to drop some of its

---

[31] Gary speaks about this in his book „Jab, jab, jab, right hook" on page 94.

products if they are not satisfied with how they are doing. Google Buzz, Google reader, Picnik, Picasa, Gmail chat became Hangouts, maybe that will go next, like Google+ recently.

YouTube has become the number one search engine and it seems to me that it is also becoming a number one social network. There are a lot of YouTubers who earn their money just by making videos. But before you go running creating a channel ask yourself is filming and planning content something you enjoy doing. If not, maybe you're not the right person for it, because your audience will notice your lack of enthusiasm. This doesn't mean you shouldn't try and see the reactions. Maybe you discover that you and your audience enjoy this kind of communication. No platform will make you a charismatic person, but maybe it can give you a chance to transform in a moment if you like to act at all, like I had a chance when I was on my Oratory exam. I was talking normally with my professor and his assistants and when the exam speech came I started projecting through the whole room.

Let's start with something that we often forget when we think about YouTube and that is that it is also some kind of a profile, but some forget to fix their profile page and make it attractive. You will do that by making a promo video that will present your channel, have a cover photo that is on topic with your subject, make playlists that will cover various subject, create a great description of the channel, clasify it, add all your social media and your website. In all of these things use as many of the keywords related to your channel as you can. If you have some sort of a release schedule, then you can write when your videos can be expected.

For you or me these may be ludacris videos and you may think to yourself who in their right mind is watching this, but someone is. This can be your driving force also, no matter what someone else thinks of something, there is always someone who will find it good or interesting. Whatever content you put out if you are following the best practices to drive visits your audience will tell you if it is good or bad, but don't say no to yourself for them.

Some of these YouTubers are also called influencers and they can do a review for you. Some you may need to pay. Rather than reading about a product people tend to open a video on YouTube and multi-task something else while listening to it. Or they may want to watch unboxing, etc. Sometimes the YouTube channel doesn't need to be huge either, as micro-influencers can also carry some weight because they may not be money driven as some have become. Sometimes it will just be a regular vlogger talking about your products. And statistics show that a video is actually 53 times more likely to show in the results of a Google search than a text page.

Of course, you could always start your own channel. But this doesn't mean you shouldn't be using the influencers too, since people may consider you biased. And a book could be written about YouTube channels and best practices, but I'll try to mention a few key ones.

On your own *'specialized'* channel you will want to keep only videos you have created and only videos on a certain topic and that is the topic of your business. On your private channel you may have cat videos and such, but on your professional channel you know who your target audience is and what interests them. So in order to keep them coming back for more, subscribe and like, you will have one topic on your channel. Eventually you can add something because it's a special occasion, holiday, something going on in your life or life of a company, but keep it simple. Once you have at least two videos that touch on a certain topic, start creating a playlist. Or even with one video. So if you are dealing with women's cosmetics you can create playlists on lipstick, eye shadow, etc. You can create playlists with someone elses videos too, indirectly using the video from their channel, they get the views, but I would suggest you only make playlists from your channel because then you are the one who controls if the video gets edited or deleted.

When publishing a video never publish it to public right away. You will want to publish it as unlisted or private. You will keep it this way until you have filled all the important details in. The video doesn't go public until you have a great title, untill you have tags and a great description.

When you are thinking about the title, *think in 140 characters*. It needs to look good on Twitter and still have enough space for the link and maybe a few hashtags. At the moment of writing this Twitter is actually testing the 280 character tweets. But even though you have 280 available, this doesn't mean you have to use them. Some of the users are still against this change and prefer the shorter tweets. They sometimes are handy, but Twitter has never been a platform for articles. You should also use shorter titles because you want them to look good on mobile too, which are happily (at least in this sense) getting bigger by the day.

Whatever you can think of that describes your video, put it in *the tags*. If it's a video about hair loss you will put in: hair, hair loss, baldness, male pattern baldness, rogaine, hair growth shampoo, hair treatment. Add at least 10 tags and if you can think of any others, use all the space you have. You will need to make *a good description of the video*. This is very important because when people search Google or when they post the video it will have the description beneath it sometimes. This description may be what drives people to the video, so the first few lines must convince them to do so. Use keywords in the first two lines. In the description, but after the clever few lines, you will *add time links*. A time link is a time stamp where you say that on 0:53 you are talking about this topic and on 2:14 you are talking about another one. This way people will skip to the content they are interested more in and text in your videos is a great thing. It is easy to add these, just write the time, no special skills or tags are needed. Only at the bottom of the description will you add where the viewers can *like or follow you*. When you are filming your video you will most likely have written some sort of an article as your script. Use it to *transcribe your video*. SEO (Search Engine Optimizer) and similar tools and behind the scenes processes love text and they usually rate better. Bonus advice: when uploading a video *don't upload it with a title video 1*, give it the title that will be the title on YouTube.

To avoid clickbait reports use accurate pictures and titles of the video.

A good tool that could help you with checking which tasks you have done and evaluating your process, but also measure which tags are giving you the best results, let you get a screen grab for a thumbnail etc. is TubeBuddy.

How to keep peoples attention? You will want to introduce the topic of your video in the first five seconds. You will say something like „Hello and welcome everyone, today we will be talking about hair loss and how to prevent it, stay tuned". Then you will give a short intro, your logo with some music and then the video starts. At the end of every video you want to ask your viewers to subscribe, like and comment. But you also want to ask them to check out your website, blog, subscribe to your newsletter. One of the newer things, I am not sure if they kept this, but YouTube asks all their creators when asking to click a link or a button bellow, to also point down in the video.

Where do you want to share your videos? EVERYWHERE. At first. One place that will remain unchanged is your own website, blog, etc. You will then make use of all the social media you can think of: Facebook, Twitter, Linkedin, Google+. You could partner up with other blogs as a contributor or a guest columnist. You will be sending at least one video with your newsletter that will build on the story you are sharing. After the initial sharing everywhere you will then make use of the YouTube analytics tool and see where you get the most return from and what websites give you the least return. This is where you will again apply the Pareto principle and see what gives you most returns and leave the rest. If you find that a certain website only gives you 1 visitor on your video, then you don't have to share there anymore.

Once you have enough content which you are the exclusive owner of you can qualify for the Content ID on YouTube. Once you do, YouTube will be able to check if someone is using your content and prevent people from possibly monetizing your own videos. This feature will also allow you to prevent showing of certain videos in certain countries.

Once your channel has grown enough and you catch peoples attention you may get approached by an MCN (Multi Channel Network). They will offer you more exposure, collaboration with other YouTubers and some other pretty things. But keep in mind that this is actually very similar to people selling you some pyramid-like system like life insurance, etc. The question you need to ask them and yourself is what can they do for you that you can't do for yourself. The answer is usually nothing and you may even end up losing revenue instead of gaining it. So be careful. And if you're ever tempted to join an MCN then try to negotiate better terms and a trial period to see how they will be helping you before you sign anything. Since you may end up losing views or revenue because they are tending to their more popular members you should also consider asking about accountability – who will be at fault if that happens. In your contract you will want to state that brand deals will only count if they fit into your channel. There is no way you can fit a PlayStation in a channel about cosmetics.

If you want to monetize your channel, I hope that you will not use too many commercial breaks. You can monetize even with only banners at the bottom of your video without interruptions and without losing your audience.

Except for the monetization on VidCon 2019 YouTube announced several new ways to make money and those include the support from your audience. First they added super chat and now they announced super stickers. These functions can only be used on live videos and they are inspired by Twitch. Except for the obvious support your audience gives you, super chat is also a way to get your attention if someone watching the video wants his question answered which would maybe get lost in an active chat. There are also various membership levels. To activate memberships you need to have 30,000 subscribers and if you are a gaming channel, then 1,000 subscribers. One of the programs is introducing sales directly over

YouTube, like T-shirts, mugs, etc. There are many websites YouTube supports, one of which is Etsy.

Snapchat is probably something you could describe as YouTube lite. It has some of the publishing features, but is more mobile friendly and you publish your video in seconds. While YouTube is great for publishing something like an episode, Snapchat can be great for shorter comunication, giving shout-outs, posting short updates of an event you are visiting or hosting, etc. The thing is that Instagram has been evolving and added something similar to this, but consumed in a different way. Snapchat is an application that is used for a less polished material with all the filters, scenarios etc. This is a place where you will be natural and, if need be, ugly. ☺ Snapchat is somewhat better for establishing a connection between a CEO and the buyer, for the personal brand. More than it is used for marketing. Which is why Snapchat isn't used by 76% of marketers. Which is a shame, because Snapchat is in top 10 of the applications for a very long time. Maybe the biggest problem with Snapchat is the lack of hashtags which help us discover people we may like. This is one of the reasons why we use the ghost frame picture to share them on other platforms and get attention on our Snapchat.

Instagram has also become a tool for marketing. Again, you may not be able to do what you can on some other sites, but for one, it always gets some new features, and second, you do not want to miss on an opportunity to have one more space you can put your website on. The more social media sites contain your web address the wider audience will be driven to it. Instagram can help you reach a larger younger female audience. Instagram has recently announced an idea that they will not show how many likes you have, which will become an issue for influencers, not so much for private accounts.

Instagram has some similarities to Twitter. Instead of being text oriented, Instagram focuses on pictures and enhancing your skill. But Twitter sometimes uses its hashtags a bit ironically and it is advised to use them sparingly there. While you can go all out on hashtags on Instagram and not go wrong. It even helps you keep your description as clean as you want and you can place your extra hashtags in the comments, rather than the description. The problem with this is that the tags get abused and you can find pictures of a car in #catsofinstagram.

Instagram is a platform that marketers want to learn more about how to advertise and they want to do more of it. Instagram is ahead of Facebook by 3 points at 72%. In 2019 69% marketers are investing more in Instagram activities.

On Instagram it is good to establish a theme. Theme doesn't have to mean only the things you photograph, it can be colors that you use, filters that you use, way you post your photographs – as singles, several pages in one or as a grid. Patek Philippe has a great Instagram profile using only the grid. The 4x3 grid looks like you are looking at their catalogue.

If you don't have too much time to post on Instagram, some of the applications that let you publish a grid have options to schedule when you want to publish something and you could set-up a week of pictures in a day.

I haven't been testing the business Instagram, but once you have a company you should have that Instagram as well, you can connect it with your page on Facebook. Using this Instagram you will also be able to sell some things.

Pinterest is very similar to Instagram, but has some key differences too. Rather than to share your moments in life on Instagram, Pinterest was invented with the goal to give you a place where you could keep the collection of your pictures, sorted in different topics. So, Pinterest is now what cutting out newspapers and magazines and keeping different hair styles and products in a file was several years ago. And because of this, it is mostly a female oriented platform. „A survey by Steelhouse shows that Pinterest users are 79% more likely to purchase something they spot on Pinterest than on Facebook. Pinterest produces four times the revenue-per-click of Twitter."[32]

Some of this data is a bit older, granted, but I wouldn't dismiss it anyway. Like Twitter hashtags, you can make use of various tags, names, descriptions. Even when you're not pinning your own content, you could tie it together with a comment that it looks better, tastes better or something else when using your product and the one you shared. And it is very important to use pinnable quality pictures and to have them lead to a link you want them to. Be sure the link is in perfect order and not 404.

Tumblr is also one of the decent platforms to try out and see if it resonates with you and if it is converting for you. On their page they say „Tumblr is so easy

---

[32] G. Vaynerchuk, Jab, jab, jab, right hook, Harper Collins Publishers, 2013, pg. 119

to use that it's hard to explain". If I would try to explain it, I'd say it's a combination of a blog, Twitter and Pinterest. This is also one of the tools that you can link with your website blog and have new posts automatically just published there. I caution you to not use that for the same reason as anything else – you don't want people following you that it's all automated, neglected and doesn't have your attention. It is actually a surprise that Tumblr is still alive, having been bought by Yahoo! who mostly buyed companies for the talent. Let's hope this is another bad decision by Yahoo! and that Tumblr will live a little longer, now owned by Verizon.

Podcast is not a platform, but a way of communicating with people. This is something like internet radio, you could make your show as a short monologue or you could invite someone to be your guest and do an interview. So why are podcasts good? They are especially good for entrepreneurs because this is a way of consuming that doesn't require your full attention. Rather, you can only listen to it, while YouTube requires you (mostly) to watch the video as well. YouTube engages your ears and your eyes, while podcasts only engage your ears and while you are listening to something you can still read or write something else. This is, actually, the way I have been consuming YouTube for years now, as some sort of quasi-podcast and this freed a lot of my time. Too bad I didn't have the vision to see that many other people would like to do several things at once or that radio could make a comeback.

SoundCloud, although at first a platform for sharing music, is one of the services you could use for your podcast. Some of the others are: buzzsprout, castos, PodBean, Podiant, Spreaker, Simplecast, blubrry. The problem is that these are paid platforms because you need hosting for your audio and bandwidth. Many have some sort of a free service, but the hosting of the files will be limited to a certain period of time and the time you can upload will also be limited. As far as I could see is that PodBean isn't bad and it seems to be the cheapest version – 9 USD per month if you pay for 12 months in advance or 14 USD monthly.

TikTok is something between Snapchat and Vine. A platform which lets you share 15 seconds short videos, which can have added sound effects. This is, however, maybe more suited for creating your personal brand than it is for advertising, but after you reached certain followers and have used hashtags smartly you could use it to announce before you do it anywhere else that your company will release a certain product. Currently this platform is inhabited by a very young population, but what you need to know is that that young population will become 18, 20 and 30 year olds and it wouldn't be bad if you got to know them now. Adjust your content to be a little bit immature.

TikTok could have some issues and it seems like it is losing some users because it is not "growing up" with them. If users grow out of this platform they could start losing them drastically. Another TikTok threat is that Facebook started working back in 2018 on its own platform which is a TikTok copy – Lasso. *Lasso* is for now available only in the USA and it seems to be a simpler version, but Facebook certainly doesn't lack the money which they could throw its way to provide some kind of a jumping board. Slingshot and Poke, also under Facebook, weren't successful as stand-alone applications, so it is for now left to follow and see how they will do with this new application and if they will succeed in taking back the group of users which they have started losing, as we mentioned earlier.

Social bookmarking sites are another kind of social communities. On these websites, like Stumbleupon and Reddit, users do not share with friends or followers, but bookmark a link to a certain thread, sub-reddit. This way people can visit these threads and follow them as a collection of similar content on one website where people can engage, comment and rate the bookmarked links.

And the next one I just mentioned... ***That is your website.*** In the beginning it can be some free placeholder website, but once you start doing this seriously, you really want to invest in something that won't give people a feeling it's done in 30 minutes and with names of the place that is hosting it in the address.

The website name needs to be your companies name or a shorter derivative of it, you do not want a website name that is as long as a whole sentence. Your website also has to have some elements and you need to acknowledge the person working for you. Websites do not cost 20 USD to get made, the good ones are a bit more expensive and if you want it working for you and earning you money, you will pay a person who knows what 'above the fold' means, what is a 'call to action' or a 'BOB'. 'Above the fold' has its origins in the newspapers and it means that when you fold the newspaper in half (yes, they used to be printed on paper) the most important information was in the top half. This is now applied to webpage design and it means that the important things are visible in the window and that you need to scroll down for the less important things. 'BOB' is a Big Orange Button and a research has shown that the color orange is the one that gets you the most clicks, not green or any other color.

The website should also have something called a *landing page*, also known as *lead capture page*. A landing page isn't necessarily visible in the links on the website, but something you create to lead somewhere to advertise further your book, promote an offer or give away some information for an exchange of contact information. You can have more than one landing page.

While leading your website and creating the content, most likely on a Blog, you will be able to create something else for your eventual landing page. So, instead of offering your expertise which you may have already translated into a book, you can also create an e-book as an anthology to your content – collect blog posts in one place, do some minor adjustments and translate it into an e-book. If the anthology way is too much, you can always do the *best of*.

Depending on the traffic you expect you will need a more expensive plan or if you do not expect too much, that is where you will save money. Your website should also be 'responsive', which means it has to be tablet and smartphone friendly. There really shouldn't be any other templates around anymore, but you never know.

As soon as you publish your website you want to have one feature on it that launches with it and not later and that is your ***e-mailing list.*** There are entrepreneurs who admit that one of their biggest mistakes was not making the list on time, which is right away. The other mistake people make with the mailing list is that they did not utilize it on time. If people subscribe to your mailing list you want to have them confirm the subscription, after that you want to send them their first newsletter. After that you shouldn't wait for too long to send another one so people wouldn't forget about you and consider you a spammer. Even though this could be seen as a little bit archaic, this is the one constant that you will always have at your disposal. Both Facebook and YouTube had some larger changes in their policies and algorithms and prices. Facebook advertising price is growing all the time, Google is changing its algorithms, the only thing that will never change is the messages that you send.

Even a smaller e-mail list is more important than a social media website. Let's face it, you can click like or follow on something just because you liked a book, movie or follow a person for whatever reason. But this isn't very personal and doesn't really mean much, except for your ego and vanity. And platforms like that can always implode, change policy, start charging for services... A mailing list is a more personal and a direct way of reaching people who have committed to you by entering their e-mail information and who want to hear from you if you have news to share.

We mistakenly believe that the e-mails we send are free. Actually, every message, every bad advertisement, every clumsy word or rushed text can cost us our client. A good practice for an e-mail list is that you do not make it look like a sales pitch and more like a regular e-mail or a letter. Here you will be using the persons name when addressing them. Your e-mail will start with 'Hello, Name' or something similar and finish with a greeting and sign your name.

Organize giveaways. Giveaways give you a chance to get so much more coverage than you usually would. If you organize a giveaway on the internet there are ways to give people more than one entry. They could earn 1 entry for liking your Facebook page, 1 entry for sharing the post on Facebook, 1 entry for following you on Twitter, 1 entry for retweeting your post, 1 entry for subscribing to your YouTube channel, 1 entry for following you on Instagram. Then you can allow them to come back every 24 hours and earn more entries by sharing those posts again until the end of the giveaway. This way you could actually have people sharing your post every day for 15-30 days. One possibility is to reward the best picture with your products. If you collect pictures for a period of time and then when you make an album invite people who have participated to invite family and friends to like the pictures, that's also another kind of exposure.

Why do giveaways give you more coverage than you would usually get? Because everyone wants free stuff, so even people who are not in your original group of the target audience will take part and you are now engaging even their friends. Because, there really is no such thing as something for nothing. They are "working" for you, promoting you through their social media, they are your promotor for a day or a month.

I will only mention the *news portals*. You will be sending a few articles to your local, but also international portals. Your local portal may consider this news and will publish it as a story on a news portal also, but international portals will eventually publish it on a portal dealing exclusively with cosmetics or if a news portal has a lifestyle section or something similar.

While you're sending e-mails to news portals, go ahead and also *contact some bloggers/YouTubers* that are covering your field of interest. Here's the issue with people contacting bloggers. It actually happens often and people who contact them aren't really a selective bunch, just out to get any attention they can. You do not contact bloggers and YouTubers who are covering gaming to talk about your make-up line. You DO NOT just ask for something from them and give nothing in return. These people actually can get paid quite nicely if they know what they are doing. They are not a charity organization. What you need to do is *solve their problem*. Once you have solved their problem and delivered them content their readers may actually like, give their audience a discount maybe, you have taken away the stress of thinking about that week's post. Gary Vaynerchuk talks about this in his book *"Jab, jab, jab, right hook"*, or as he translates it, *"Give, give, give, ask"*.

QR code... is probably the most ignored and forgotten tool in the book, even though it is relatively new. QR code may not have the biggest ROI (Return on Investment), but it is something you can place anywhere and it can lead to any content. You can make it to lead to your electronic business card, to your website, to your video. And now the QR code can even be designed to your own preference, it can have your logo in the middle of it, you can change its colour and the edges. There are many possibilities. Like I said, the ROI may not be great, but if the investment is not huge I wouldn't leave any stone unturned.

Subscriptions are slowly making their way into internet sales. Companies are using the subscription model to help the people think less about when they need to make a certain purchase. You do not need to go to the store anymore to see if they have something you need. Even worse, if they just ran out of something. What happens here is that once people buy from you, they then set-up a date when they would usually make the next purchase and from then on it is recurring. What can happen is that people can also pause, skip or cancel. What you can do then is contact those people if they did not order for 3 months and ask them what you could do better to have their business back. The usual great title is "We miss you" or something along those lines. You could offer them a discount for coming back. You could also offer discounts as some sort of reward if they stay your customer for a certain period of time. Most of the time discount is the preferred reward for the customers, but you could also add something special for annual rewards – either the birthday of your company, where you can offer rewards to your current subscribers at the same time, or anniversary of each individual subscriber for that month, which is a little bit harder to track.

Use *live video* as your marketing tool. Live video is present on Facebook, YouTube, Twitch, Periscope... This is a type of marketing that is on an upward trajectory. Instead of prepared speeches and presentations, this way your customers get to see the real and unedited you.

Webinars, coming from words 'web' and 'seminar', are also a good tool to use for marketing. Doing an online seminar is a great way of establishing credibility with your audience, give some information for an exchange of creating a relationship.

Search Engine Optimization or SEO is last, but not the least in our internet marketing segment. Having an SEO optimized website means that your website has some keywords and other elements that make it more popular with search engines, so it ranks up higher in search results. One of the ways you will be achieving this will be link building. Do not expect to be number one on Google search the day you start the website, but it can happen. It is good to have a blog on the website so it keeps refreshing and doesn't get recognized as "stale". Don't think there's such an expression in SEO terminology, just trying to get a point across.

While you're adding this content to your blog you will want to do several things. You will most likely use some pictures for your content and as a featured image that appears when one shares your post on the social media. Name those pictures. Do not have some random name or a number sequence. Add tags to the post you are writing. When writing a post you can refer to a post you made earlier by saying something like "As we discussed in the post about…". This way you are giving the user a reason to stay longer on your website and creating interest in another article of yours. All of this is taken in consideration when rating the website. You will want as many links as possible leading to your content: from social media and other websites (external) and from one post to another (internal). When adding a link that doesn't lead to your website, keep it at the bottom of the article. If you are writing about someone else, write your article and then at the end mention "If you would like to check out and follow so and so then you can visit his or her website and twitter". This way you don't have people leaving your website one sentence in the article.

You will also strengthen your SEO optimization by using some keywords in your title, in the body of your article, excerpt, tags… Wherever you can. To check what words are looked up by what audiences you could use Google Keyword Planner or Keyword Tool. Some preference is also given to the sites with SSL encryption, which is easiest to recognize by the additional 's' in the https:// part of the web address.

One thing you need to be aware of when you are using internet for marketing is *feedback*. You will never be able to please everyone and address everyone's needs and desires, so you must be ready and even expect for people to leave comments and feedback you may not like. No product is 100% great and flawless. The feedback might be very bad sometimes. But you do not want to filter

71

those out or censor them in any way, unless they are using a language nobody really should be using. Some people want to see only positive feedback on their websites and products, but the fact of the matter is that those can look like they are fake or paid for. Occasional negative feedback gives that much more merit to the positive ones.

3.6.2 Classic marketing

Be honest. Jack Welch calls this the biggest dirty little secret in business. This is not something you will see too much in business advice. But try and do this as best as you can. Why so? Because, for one, I would like to start promoting an entrepreneur who isn't cutthroat. I am trying to be that and I want to invite you to represent a conscientious and honest kind of entrepreneur, one who doesn't cave in, lowers standards or gives up because the rest is doing things badly. The kind that, when we're speaking of the cosmetic industry, does not use the 100% paraben free stamp as a marketing trick and then has all kinds of different bad ingredients. Even Immanuel Kant believed that when people avoid candour in order to stay in good favour with other people, they actually destroy trust, and in that way, they ultimately erode society. Or, in our case, a business. And, of course, it is very refreshing to see an honest entrepreneur and being that you become more likeable, being likeable people trust and respect you more, etc.

The other reason is that when you are honest with your clients you will not give them anything to doubt you for or challenge you. When a company says something like "Avis is only No. 2 in rent-a-cars" it doesn't leave you any room to attack it, but you come to the understanding that it is good, because there are who knows how many of those companies. "You have to prove a positive statement to the prospect's satisfaction. No proof is needed for a negative statement."[33] When using this you do need to be careful, because the negative statement that you would be using needs to be widely known and not just in some closed circle of the company. Also, when stating the negative you want to have a fast 'but statement', not apologizing, but pointing to the positive. "The taste you hate, twice a day. Listerine."

The customers also need to experience your sincerity and that you are interested in solving their problems and not only turning profit. And this can't be faked. Your selling process will be the one talking for you also. I have experienced a telephone call where a company that I get my internet from is offering another

---

[33] A. Ries, J. Trout, The 22 immutable laws of marketing, HarperCollins Publishers, 1993., p. 89

service to me as their longstanding customer over many years. They only opened their office where I live not even a year ago. So, another advice here to not use your practiced sales speech.

Business cards are probably one of the first and smallest investments you will make. For introducing yourself and establishing credibility while providing people with your contact details it is good to have these. Business cards can hold many details, but I wouldn't suggest cluttering them up. Just the most important details is fine.

Business cards today can be made virtually from any material and designed into any shape or form, so if you are a hairdresser you may as well make a business card that looks like a comb. Having a higher quality material and print and actually being interesting is a great feature for a business card.

Another two tricks are usefulness and how you present your card. You may want to make a card useful. In the past people were putting calendars on the back of the cards, but now when somebody needs a calendar, they usually reach for their phone, not the card. So maybe there is something else closely related to your business that you could use. Another trick is to present the card properly and not like you were handing them to some guy in the street you know from high school. For example, if you are giving a business card to a Japanese national, the proper way of doing this is holding the card by the corners with both hands, the information facing the other person so they can read the card even while you're holding it and with a slight bow. Showing etiquette will only make a better impression of you and your company.

This is something not all of us have. That's *friends in the media* that can set us up with being a guest in a show. But even if you don't, you may send an e-mail to your TV and radio station. These stations are always on the lookout for the news and content. They may invite you as a guest to talk once about your product. Or you could address them as a content creator and treat it almost like a version of a YouTube channel. There you will be considered an expert in your field answering a few questions, telling your story, maybe taking calls together with the host.

Speaking of media, you could *make use of printed media*. You could reach out to newspapers that could feature a story on how you started your business. Right next to that page you could buy an advertisement. You could also reach out to magazines that you believe your target audience is reading and eventually you could have a sample of your product in that magazine. You need to understand one thing. Rarely will someone jump to your help when you ask them to solve your problem. But when you solve their problem and give them a way to make their magazine richer that month, then you may open some doors for yourself.

What you need to know about the "old media" is that its value is really diluting. Maybe value is a wrong word, but definitely impact. Years ago you would have become famous just for being on one show and being featured in one of very few big newspapers. Now, in the era of social media and when you can communicate with your audience directly, this changes. Still, I am not saying you shouldn't make use of any possible marketing you can think of, but I do want you to be aware of the changes that have happened and that are still happening. The old media isn't necessarily bad, but don't be surprised of the impact it does.

Speaking of media... One more strategy you could use is ***newsjacking***. Comes from words *'news'* and *'hijacking'*. This strategy is similar to the trending hashtags on Twitter. What you would be doing is follow the news and when you see something that relates to you or your business, you would insert yourself into that conversation. If somebody reports that someone has done something first and you know you were that person, then you use that to send correct information and get coverage. But, also, you can use whatever news is trending at that moment. It may be worth noting that newsjacking is referred to as earned media because you need to hustle to get it. As opposed to advertising, sponsorships, etc., which are paid media.

Even though we may not have many friends in the media, we still have access to one simple tool that doesn't require much effort – ***pamphlets***. Even if you have international aspirations you should always include your local community which may want to support you because they know you or because there's something new and good at their doorstep.

Price can also be used as a marketing tool in more ways than one. Not only for discounting the original price, but you could also promote that your price is fair and that you have the best interest of your buyers in mind. Some products will have on the packaging how much the production of the product cost, how much everything else cost and how much the company earns. This way forming an honest relationship with the buyer.

Of course, if you want to be like the companies who spend cents and ask for tens of dollars for their products I don't suggest you use this approach. You could, however, point out that your customers are buying a superior product for a cheaper price. 'Cheap' doesn't need to mean that it has the lowest possible price, even though cosmetics are really overpriced, because you don't want to appear to be cheap. By this we mean you don't want anyone to think that you have the cheap quality.

Outdoor displays can take various forms. They can be large billboards, smaller posters, bumper stickers, signs on a bus or a truck, banners, etc. With this kind of advertising you will want to engage people where you think they'll be buying.

Having *branded items* such as T-shirts, hats, pens, pencils, lighters, USB sticks, etc. isn't a bad idea... if you have some money burning a hole in your pocket. The issue I have with this is that these items rarely end up being used and seen by more people. Maybe some of them.

Speaking of which, *engage with your community*. You could make a public stand and allow them to test your products. You will engage with them as a charismatic person you are and help them determine what product they need and want. You could be making skin and hair care and styling products. So test some of the products on the spot. If you have a shampoo, get those hotel-sized shampoo bottles and let them take it home to try it out.

And that brings us to another one. *Have some sample sized products*. Maybe your products will be too expensive to buy the whole product right away. Maybe the people will not trust your product right away because they are using a name they know about. You could even have a face cream sample act like your business card, with all the info on it. And with the sample sizes, when someone orders a certain amount of products and you still have some they did not order, include those so they can test those products and maybe buy them next time around.

The size of the sample sized products isn't really reflected in their price. The price will not be drastically lower for a fraction of an amount of your regular product, but your margin should cover you enough that you aren't losing money on these samples and there is a big possibility that you may get people to buy something they didn't in the first place.

Please be aware of the presentation of your samples. The packaging of these is also essential, as they are your marketing product. I once purchased a shaving cream and received something extra... I can't even call it a sample. It looked like some extra product got scraped from the bottom and sent to a customer. I was so intrigued by this that I even sent a message to the seller to check what this was. It didn't look attractive, didn't look sanitary, so I threw it into the trash. Never ordered anything again from this business. What would you call this?

Do NOT send your trash as sample products. Either have them or don't.

While engaging with your community you could also ***sponsor*** a local small sports team. This isn't in your wheelhouse, but it shows your presence. Or you could find an event that has something to do with you and be one of the sponsors for it. There people who use cosmetics for a living will be able to work with your products, test them and possibly recommend them, even buy them for themselves.

You could also ***give guarantees.*** For instance, you may want to offer a refund in a set number of days if a customer doesn't like your product, but be careful, you do not want to have a used product shipped back to you, so what you would be doing is shipping a small sample tester product which your customer could try out and reach a decision to keep the product or not.

Guarantees can be used to either compel people or to filter them out. You may compel people to try your product in case they feel safe that they aren't throwing their money away. "Nev Lapwood, who runs a snowboarding instruction program (…) offers a 120 percent guarantee. If the program doesn't rock your world, you'll get 100 percent of your money back, *plus* 20 percent for your trouble."[34] In case you choose not to offer any guarantees you may use this as a filter and have only clients who are a good fit for you, while steering those who aren't away.

---

[34] C. Guillebeau, The $100 Startup, Crown Publishing, 2012., p. 123

Never forget your current customers. Very often in some lines of business you will see companies giving some offers to new customers. So you should now cancel your phone and get a new one? No, you shouldn't. It's the same with your customers. While you want to attract new ones, also offer a certain discount or something else to show the ones still loyal to you how much you appreciate them. Here we could mention something called "grandfathering". This means that while you may increase your price for your new customers or subscribers, you keep the price for the customers who have been with you since the start when you had lower prices.

Upselling is something that can make you money, but not something I would advise you use too aggressively, since it can also cost you money if you go too far. What is upselling? This is when you come to a restaurant and they offer you a drink or a salad with something, fries with your order in McDonald's or some other extra with your main order or your main course, shirt with a suit, tie with a shirt. If we are talking cosmetics, what could we say is a good pair? Face wash and a scrub, certain make-up and brushes, shampoo and shower gel, etc.

Word of mouth is possibly still the best kind of marketing. Whatever you do, no matter how good or expensive your marketing is, nothing is worth more than a satisfied consumer and nothing will cost you more than one who isn't.

The reason why this is true is because people may always be skeptical of the message you are trying to get across, because you have something to gain, profit. The internet is a place where you can leave a bad review every step of the way and people will find it. But people who recommend you this way do not gain anything or lose anything, which can work for their credibility, especially if they are considered to be someone who understands the subject.

People also talk to their friends and if a product leaves any strong impression on them, good or bad, they are bound to share it with someone. So, if you think that you have left a good impression and that your customer is about to leave satisfied, you can always ask them to recommend you to someone else.

It doesn't matter if you are only an internet store or if you also have a place for people to visit, a *voucher* can be a great idea. The voucher can be given in physical form at the checkout. For example, you could give a certain amount voucher for a certain amount of money spent with you. This means that you already had this customer and by giving them a voucher that should be valid from the next day, you then give that same customer an incentive to come back and visit you again, possibly do some more shopping. If this is a permanent practice and not something you do only on certain dates, this could potentially make you heaps of money. You spend something on making the vouchers, some may not cash them in, but some will come back to do that and spend another X amount of money and they could get more vouchers. It's a vicious little circle.

Own a word. This is a suggestion from *"The 22 immutable laws of marketing"*. Basically, when you think of a product or something that you need to do, you should be able to think of this word. In the USA for a long time when someone needed to make a photocopy of something they would say that they need to Xerox it. Or, if you want a more modern example, you certainly noticed that Google became a verb. Nobody says "Put it in the search engine on the internet" or "Yahoo! it" – it's "Google it!". This has become so widespread and so known by the general public that it has gone that far that the word 'google' is now in various dictionaries.

You could also own a design or a colour. Colour is a bit trickier, but what do you think when you think of Coca-Cola? Red background, white letters, I don't know if there is a different name for the Coca-Cola font, Santa Claus drinking Coke for Christmas.

But be aware of several things here. All examples here are, or at least were at their prime, huge companies – Google, Xerox, Coca-Cola. It would be very hard to own something 6 months into the business or a year. So, while I would encourage you to have the goal of owning a word, it's a long game you are playing here.

Develop your 'unique selling proposition'. This is often a short slogan for your business and it is something so simple that will even go into your unconscious mind and stay there. It is now very hard to say 'zoom zoom' and not think of Mazda, 'You can' Cannon, 'Just do it' Nike, 'I am…' Nikon. The proposition should also be followed up with something that will address the conscious mind and that will explain what you are offering. And you are not just offering a *product*, you are also offering its *result* for a certain *problem*.

Put the dates to good use. I don't want you to start doing marketing when you're out on a date, I want you to start using certain days and months to your advantage. Whenever there is a national or international day of something that you could relate to, use it. Sometimes there are even months for some causes. And there is quite a few of those to choose from. Mickey Mouse birthday, National Absurdity Day, International Ninja Day and more. I'm using these silly examples and not something like Black History Month or International Women's Day just to show how much choice you actually have and that there is a day or a month for almost anything.

3.6.3 Entrepreneurial marketing

All marketing isn't created equal. Entrepreneurial marketing is different to the marketing of established companies for one reason and one reason only – resources. These resources are both in finance and in personnel.

The financial reasons are very easy to understand. The company that is just starting up doesn't have the financial power to have huge billboards, TV commercials, celebrity ambassadors, etc. So, often new companies need to be more innovative and think outside of the box to do some marketing. They need media to speak about them because what they are doing and changing, not because they are paying them to. If you're in cosmetics and you want to ride the wave of media carrying your marketing for a while, then you will need to introduce something it is worth talking about for a while and not only use to fill the gap in while waiting for something better.

Another resource that new companies are lacking is marketing talent or personnel. Same as having lack of funds to pay for huge commercials, new companies also will not have too much money for marketing directors and whole departments dedicated just to marketing. Whereas larger companies can afford to even spend hundreds of thousands or even more just on research.

OK, I may have lied. It is also different because it is very chaotic. Instead of focusing your attention on something, in this stage we are trying to get the attention of others in every possible way, using as many tools as we can. Internet may make some things and processes easier, but in many ways it makes things harder also. We used to have some time before we had to step up our game, now with technology and social media we have to do it constantly. All the media and search engines are periodically changing their algorithms. They are doing this because the users get flooded with certain content and become numb, they don't consume it anymore and they need to make the quality of marketing they show to their users higher. And we have to fight for attention with everyone.

I hope this does not discourage you. I already covered the vast number of possibilities you can use on the internet for a small amount of money. This is only here to say that you need to not underestimate anyone you are up against and know that there are differences in marketing strategies and that to win that particular game of chess you need to be aware of the tools someone else may use and what you can use to fight for your piece of cake. You are certainly not powerless when it comes to a marketing fight of a David versus Goliath proportion, you will only need to be a little bit more creative with it.

3.6.4 Customer acquisition cost

When paying for any kind of marketing you need to keep in mind one thing. What is your *customer acquisition cost*? This is also called *conversion price*. This is the money you spent on an advert or a review and then following how many customers you got from it. If you pay 100 for an advert and get 1 customer, your conversion price is 100. And your product may cost only 10. You're losing money here. So your goal is to, ideally, keep the conversion price as low as possible.

When working with different YouTube influencers and other internet marketing options, you want to assign everyone their personal link, very much like affiliate marketing. This way you can track which marketing option actually paid off and which you shouldn't be investing in anymore.

With the customer acquisition cost also comes customer retention and customer lifetime value. *Customer retention* is simply the ability of a company to keep a customer over a period of time. *Customer lifetime value* is the expression of how much the customer spends with the company from the start of their relationship to its end. The customer lifetime value can even turn a bad customer acquisition cost into good value just if the span of time the customer stays with the company is long enough.

Sometimes companies and people will even go into the negative numbers on the acquisition cost only to get the money back on the time customer stays with the company. Subscription-based businesses will want customers to stay with the company for a longer period of time to get the money back and more. Also, larger companies will be able to sell a product for a lesser price, only to get it back on servicing cars, for example.

3.7 Online business

In today's world it becomes more and more rare to do business via the classic brick and mortar stores and often people turn to doing business online. It's more convenient and easier to find if you know what you're looking for. From the comfort of your home. Even the so-called classic stores now have a way to order some of their goods online, often on their own website, but also on websites like eBay or Amazon.

With the modern tools to create a website now everybody can have one within minutes and the plug-ins enable you to add various functions to it, such as e-commerce plug-ins for sales. What you do need to know is that for people to trust a website, especially one they put their credit card information in, the website needs to have a certain level of security, protection and certificates to prove such.

After people have ordered your goods, you will also need to deliver those. To be able to deliver your goods you will need to have a certain relationship with companies that deliver packages for you. It can be regular post or maybe you have an account with a company that offers more safety and better ways to track your items. Regular post is pretty decent and very often it will do the job that it is supposed to do. The thing is that there are some countries that may have issues with delivering the package that you have sent and it may be safer to do business with some better shipping service that will provide more safety. This may save you money (for not having to re-send the order again), but it will also save your reputation, which is more important.

For an online store, especially an online only store, you will need to address the marketing strategy accordingly. For instance, you don't advertise for online shopping on a radio or some of the older ways of marketing. If your audience is looking you up on the internet to shop with you, you will need to address the space they spend their time in, and that is the internet. So, you will need to advertise mostly on the internet. That is not to say that you will only be using the internet, your local community should also know about you and if you have anything to do with fashion you may invest in some fashion magazines, but do not expect the most ROI from those sources.

3.8 Good business practice

Apart from a good business model, you will also need to develop a good business practice. And while quality products, being polite to customers and being very good in customer service is important, there is one thing that many businesses overlook. This one shares the first place with customer service and customer value.

Underpromise, overdeliver. This basically means that you should never put yourself in the position that you promise something to your customer that you can not deliver. This can be delivery time, response time that you promised in your automatic e-mail when someone contacts you, quality, cost, quantity... Everything you can think of. If you think the delivery of your order will last 7 days, then promise at least 10, maybe even more. "Render more and better service than you are paid for, and sooner or later you will receive compound interest from your investment. It is inevitable that every seed of useful service you sow will sprout and reward you with an abundant harvest."[35]

You will not lose customers if they know from the start the time frame their product will get delivered, but you will definitely win them if the item gets there sooner than expected. And you may actually lose them if you're told that the delivery will last 5-7 days and then they wait for a month. Be realistic, actually, be even pessimistic when you promise, but carry out the promise like an optimist.

The sooner you figure some of these things out, the better it will be for your business. Another one of these is *what business are you in and what is your product*. Many people, when asked what they do or sell, will answer that they are in the „skin care business" or „IT business" or something else. You do not sell a hand cream, nor is that your product. Your biggest product is your company, your business. You are your biggest product. The business and the way it is ran and the values it represents may even be equally if not more important than the commodity you sell. So, what you are selling is not a hand cream, it's a promise of a soft and caring touch that will be important when meeting the love of your life, or the confidence of having clean and taken care of hands when sealing a deal with a partner. The commodity you are selling may be a shampoo, but you are not selling a shampoo, you are selling, in case it is for hair growth, hope and confidence, happiness, fulfilment.

Value is a business practice you cannot afford to not give. And many businesses fail to give it because they fail to define it. Often people and businesses think that the value of something is its price before the discount or something along the lines of that. But this is wrong.

---

[35] N. Hill, Keys to Success, The 17 Principles of Personal Achievement, Penguin Group, 2007, p. 63

The value you give to your customers cannot be only material. This value needs to be perceived by the customer and registered on an emotional level, not by checking the price of what they are getting. The value must come in the form of appreciation of your customers. This will be evident in your customer service. This will be evident in the small gifts you provide when they are buying from you. It will be evident in the carefully packaged product. A photographer who takes it one step further will send a card congratulating the anniversary to the couple he was shooting on their wedding day and offer them a discount if they wish to do something else. A value is a smile when someone enters and leaves your shop, a nice word. "Starting out in a simple shoe store in 1920s in Seattle, the Nordstrom family has built a chain of department stores famous around the country for service and willingness to bend over backward to please their customers. A garment may be return any time it fails to satisfy, even years after the original purchase. Sales associates will call branches all across the country to find an item in the size and color a customer wants. One woman even sent a Mother's Day card on behalf of the customer who mentioned that she had forgotten to do so."[36]

Probably the biggest value you can give to your customer is the feeling of being heard. This is not just customer service, this is any interaction. Remember that if you have done something wrong the customer could just ignore you and never come back again. Them reaching out to you in any way should be rewarded with the feeling of being heard. They cared so much about an issue that they have found it necessary to contact you and you should not be dismissing this. You should actually value it very much. Even if the wording in the e-mail or comment or whichever type of communication is strong, harsh and borderline insulting, you can still find something of value for you and your business in there. Not everything that is good for you comes in a wax sealed letter and kind words, like you just got invited to Hogwarts. Or as Bill Gates put it, "Your most unhappy customers are your greatest source of learning".

"The truth about customers is that they will tell you what they *don't* want."[37] Or as Benedict Cumberbatch playing Sherlock Holmes put it, "People don't like to tell you things, but they love to contradict you".

---

[36] N. Hill, Keys to Success, The 17 Principles of Personal Achievement, Penguin Group, 2007, p. 65
[37] B. Schroeder, Fail Fast or Win Big, AMACOM, 2015, p. 96

It is also important to know that the value is individual. You will show great appreciation to your customers by doing these things, but they will not perceive it at the same value. Some may think the world of what you have done, while others may find very little value, but they will still recognize the care and appreciation. And this is the point where you can shape the *customer truth*. Customer truth is something that a customer believes to be true. And what the customer doesn't perceive to be a reality and truth, then it isn't. And because the customer isn't necessarily always right, but they are never wrong, you want to listen to this and try to shape it, if possible. Customers have stopped using services and buying products for the smallest of issues after service quality

Because of this value, which is given freely, you will also be able to charge more and your customers will still enjoy doing business with you because this is your product – you make them feel special. And customers remember the service much longer than they remember the price.

Value isn't something that you should show only to your customers, either, you should also show it to your partners and employees. You can't expect people to work in your best interest, if you don't think of theirs. If you, by chance, end up earning millions, you can't keep paying your people nickles and dimes. That is the monetary side of value, the other side is that you remember their names. OK, I know you won't start with 100 different people, so that shouldn't be too hard, but even if you are not social with them, you could try and remember something about their lives. Maybe something about their children or spouse, ask how that something went, etc.

You never know what one small act of random kindness can do and what kind of lasting impression it can leave. In the movie *Evan Almighty* Morgan Freeman who is playing God in the movie (who else?) after he is asked by Evan (Steve Carell) to give him strength to change the world, he asks him to build an ark. At the end of the movie we find out what the ark actually was. ARK – Act of Random Kindness. Gary Vaynerchuk is telling a story in one of his videos how he posted on Twitter that people could send him their number and he would call them. The ones who had no issues with privacy sent their number and he called a few people. After that one person said on Twitter that "it didn't take Gary much time, but now I am an advocate for life"[38].

---

[38] A compilation of some of his statements you can see at https://youtu.be/lluAImMVqFA

While getting this feedback from your customers and providing them with a feeling of being heard, you will also need to ***learn to deal with negative feedback***. There are four stages of turning negative feedback into a positive experience: acknowledge, analyze, respond and apologize, resolve.

In practice it should look something like this:

Hello,

Thank you for contacting our customer service. We understand that you are having issues with some of our services/products.

We have looked into the problem you have described and we have found what the issue was. We apologize for the inconvenience and any frustration this may have caused you, this problem should be fixed now. (Alternatively, you could say that you are aware of the issue and are working on resolving it and expect it to be finished at estimated time, never ASAP. Another alternative is to give the customer the steps how to solve the issue they are having, in case it's something that only can be fixed on their end.)

Please accept this 20% discount for your next purchase with our company.

Sincerely,

Davor

There are some angry people on the internet and sometimes it will be a challenge to write something like this. But rather than to ignore the customer, making them even angrier or to respond fiercely, you need to stay calm. This way you will show that you are a responsive company and that you place value on your customers and other people reading this will see how you handle negative feedback. So, if you handle negative that well, how will you handle good feedback? Plus, you will seem like a bigger person, avoiding conflict and someone else will have the bad image. You could even take that as a compliment, as some say that you did not make it until someone hates you.

Social responsibility is something entrepreneurs of all sorts tend to put to the very back and often not even touch on it. Even on seminars of eminent entrepreneurs this is given the minimum thought and time, if any. As a successful person your moral values should push you to give to those who are less fortunate, support your community, invest in others, etc. And I really hope that you are this person. If you are not, you would still be wise to be socially responsible, because this is also a form of marketing. While you are doing good, you are also getting eventually your logo or a banner of some kind shown on the events you are supporting and your name is usually mentioned in the news when announcing the event and on posters, etc.

You will also need to *learn how to contact people.* When I write this it seems like it's obvious, what would I have to say here at all? Quite a bit that I don't see people do very often. Two main things, though.

- If you are calling someone over the telephone and there is a chance they may not have your number, you will always introduce yourself. If you had prior contact the introduction would be shorter, if you didn't have prior contact or it was too brief, the information would be longer.
- E-mailing is another issue. I don't like to see when people want to explain the whole history of everything in the first e-mail. Make the first e-mail as short as possible. Introduce yourself and ask in as few words as possible if you could send a proposition for a project, business, whatever. Maybe the person you are e-mailing doesn't have the time to spend reading two pages of your explanation and maybe you're not e-mailing the right person anyway, so they will give you where to address your e-mail. The first e-mail is never about pitching, *but establishing contact and familiarity.* People will sooner read and answer to a shorter e-mail than a long one and if they don't answer anyway, then you wasted less of your time.

This last one isn't so much about the business, but it is about you and the role you occupy in your business. When building a business, that doesn't mean that you are staying in it forever. Maybe you are building it with an exit strategy and aim to sell it for high profit. You should ***always have a nice title for your position in your company***. So, you should be a CEO, CFO, Director of… and not something trivial people wouldn't care about or even recognize. This is good to have because you want to have something for your CV if you ever need to apply for something, be it a job with a company or introduce yourself to partners, prospects, etc.

3.9 A few points about selling

When you are selling your products, you will obviously need to do marketing, place your products in stores and/or on the internet, etc. At one point or another you will be talking about what you are doing and what you are selling. You may even end up hiring people to talk to others and market your products over the phone or in person. The problem becomes how you or eventually someone else will be presenting your products. I mentioned already that my internet provider company tried to get me to get a telephone with them by using a practiced pitch. They were calling me their "customer for several years" and the company was only open for less than 12 months in the city I live in. And we all hate when something like this happens. But we are a consumer society and we buy a lot of stuff, often even stuff we don't need. So, what is the main take away from this and possibly the main point in this title? *People hate to be sold things, but they love to buy them.*

And because people love to buy, you won't need to be the salesperson. You and your company will need to be liked. If people like you and if they respect you, they will buy from you. This, of course, doesn't mean that you can lay everything else to rest. But you need to know that people often buy with their feelings, not reason. Liking often leads to trust and respect. This is true because liking forms the customer truth, even if it may not be the real truth the customers perceive it to be such.

We spoke somewhat about the branding of your company and products. When people start to like you, trust you and respect you, you will also become a part of that brand. To become a brand you will want to earn the reputation of quality, become an expert in your field, register a website domain in your name, and one of the more important ones... become a resource.

If you end up selling something, start with value. At all cost avoid "but wait, there's more" line and start with what value you are providing, then go with what it will cost people. And if you manage to pique someone's interest, you will not need to sell it anyway. They will sell it to themselves.

When you are marketing to people it is not enough just to list the products they get, you should be able to tell them why they are buying it. It is not enough to just state the characteristics of the products, you need to give a *'so that' statement.* This means that you will say something like "You will get this book" (your classic listing) "so that you can learn how to start a business and be a succesful entrepreneur". Ask questions you will get a *'yes' answer* to. This way you will filter out the customers you want and the ones you don't. If I wanted to ask a question about this book I would say something like "Have you been looking for a book about a business in cosmetics, but weren't satisfied with what is out there?". Establish *common interests.* If you are doing something in your city say something like "If you are ever in … visit us at …". A common interest can be something else too. If you can, *use numbers.* Maybe you can say that your product will reduce crows feet by 30% in a certain number of days. Use your *landing page* in your marketing. Now, this is mostly used for Facebook advertising, which isn't to say that you can't apply it somewhere else. Precise speech with intent which tells you why you need a certain product is beneficial everywhere.[39]

People often forget that whatever their line of business they are always in the service industry. It's not only in the cafe, hotel or similar industries. Same goes for everyone who at any point gets in touch with people. And you need to put value into those people and you need to make them feel it, that way you will be able to keep them as your loyal customers.

---

[39] G. Bell, 6 Facebook Ad Copy Secrets to Improve Your Conversions, Social Media Examiner, 23.07.2019. https://www.socialmediaexaminer.com/6-facebook-ad-copy-secrets-to-improve-conversions/ [Accessed: 30.07.2019.]

4 Financing

You will not be able to get into this before you start researching. Which is why this part of the book is placed so far back. In order to even start thinking about financing you will need to figure out what you want to make, how many products you want to make, what market you want to address, the complexity of your formula, if you're working with a laboratory, will also influence the price, etc. So, to even think about the price you will need to get to a point where you know what you want and begin talking to a laboratory.

So, to reiterate, if you're working with a laboratory and not making natural cosmetics you will need to send them either a formula if you're a chemist or a list of ingredients from which they will create a formula. Then their base price includes some basic testing. If you want more than those, some other tests cost more. Sometimes a laboratory will offer you a discount if you're developing more than a certain number of products with them. Sometimes they will offer you that you get a certain percentage back. There is usually a way to deal with this once you get to this stage.

If you started without funding, like I did, then this is the part that will give you the most headache. I had everything finished. The research was done. I knew my target audience, I knew what products I wanted to have, what ingredients I wanted in them, what I didn't want, I knew what would make me different from the rest, but financing wasn't in place.

What we come to realize very fast is that no idea, no matter how great it is, doesn't move anywhere without the money. You will certainly get further with an average idea and a lot of money than with a great idea and no money. Do you think you would be hearing about Apple if there wasn't a person with almost 100.000 USD?

4.1 Financing plan

The reason why I said this would give you the most headache is because at this stage you will start learning about the hidden costs of the business.

First of all, there is something called 'the cost of doing business'. This is the cost of all utilities and every essentials you need to pay to keep your doors open.

But... First you need to open the doors. So, you need to register a company. Possibly trademark the name. Then that company needs an address and the address can't be your living room. If it's cosmetics you're working with, then you may need something to properly store them. You can't only develop the product, you need to produce it and fill it into something attractive to sell it, so you need nice containers. If you're going to ship it, you need boxes. Where will those products and those boxes be stored? Now, apart from the office you also need some sort of a storage. Your server and domain will need to be paid for, you will need to pay a person taking care of it and pray to God you don't become a target of a hacker just because they got bored. If you grow and you do good marketing, you may need to change a plan for your website, so it can take a larger traffic load.

Every year (at least, probably more often) you will need to pay a bookkeeper to do your books. I don't know how it is around the world, but where I live even if you have 0 traffic on your account (which I hope you don't), you are obliged to show that in your books and pay for that. Then you need to pay your taxes. And if you're like the majority of people who do not like to pay taxes you will try to find a way to write them off, which is another kind of a headache since it feels like you're losing money, etc.

Will you be working alone or will you (which would be smarter) be working with someone else? Those people won't work for free, now you need to pay them.

Divide the expenses in two – one time expenses and monthly expenses. When you multiply the monthly expenses by 12, you get the number that you will need to keep the doord open for a year. When you add the expenses of starting the company and buying everything you need, you get a very large number, which would be great if you had it at the beginning. Actually, you could multiply it by 6 so you don't get too scared, but if it is possible, aim at longer periods. Especially when you are working in cosmetics which needs to be made, tested, approved, ordered and delivered.

In any case... This is the point where I stopped and asked myself do I want this kind of a headache. The answer, of course, is no, but we continue despite it, because we always want to change something and leave something behind.

4.2 Funding

The obvious thing here is that you want to know how much money you will need. Whichever funding option you choose, you will need to know this. For the people who would back your idea, but also for yourself. You do not want to go into this endeavour without knowing how much money you need. Raise too little and you will not have enough to finish what you started. Raise too much and you can lose credibility with your partners and have more interest you now need to return. But still be generous when you're determining those numbers, because most people forget to consider small expenses that can add up, like bank transfers. Also, you can better track a set number than an abstract one and knowing that number will show that you have an understanding of the field you are aspiring to work in.

With all these options of raising money, there is one universal truth. Make the issue personal. People may be impressed by a statistic you found about what happens to pets if they live longer than their owners or how many children get hurt in their homes. But you will get them only when you make it personal and ask them about their pets and their children and if they care what is going on with them. It's the same message, but people sometimes need it rephrased to recognize it as important. Or as George Carlin put it, "Rainforests and wetlands came into existence because the environmentalists discovered people were not willing to give money to save jungles and swamps".

So… How can you fund your start-up? Well, *you can always reach in your own pocket*. If you're in a good financial situation, you can fund your own start-up. You could cash in your credit card, you could tap into some other savings you have, but, let's face it, many of us who are only starting aren't in that kind of situation to give all sorts of money on something this large. So what are your other options?

You could ask your friends and family… Many experts do not recommend this and I wouldn't either. This is why people call this the 3F category or FFF. Because people supporting you here are friends, family and fools. While you could have friends with the financial power to do this, you do not want to lose them or get in some sort of a fight because of that. Family… Unless you can ask your father for a million dollar loan then it's probably even worse than friends. The family will be your great support, they can help you test the product and reach a verdict when you get samples from laboratories. But never work with family. And why fools? Because just like your friends and family, fools also don't really check what you are getting into and support you anyway.

You could ask for a loan. Now, please try to stay away from loan sharks, at least the illegal kind and try the legal ones. You will want to contact more than one bank to see what they can offer you. Some micro-credits can be good too, depending on how large is the sum you will be asking for.

Venture capital firms make direct investments in companies in exchange for equity stakes in the business. Venture capital is usually raised when a company has been around for a while, at least a year. Rarely for starting up from zero. „Since most venture capital firms are partnerships, they tend to be highly selective and usually invest only in businesses that are already established and have shown the ability to generate profits. Competition for venture capital funding is intense. Individual venture capital firms may receive more than 1,000 proposals a year and are mainly interested in businesses that require an investment of at least 250,000 USD.“[40]

„Industry averages show that venture capitalists invest in about one out of every 400 deals they review. While their funding levels are higher, $3 to $7 million per investment, they are extremely selective. Especially after the internet bubble of 2000 and the recession of 2008, venture capitalist firms have been hesitant to look at start-ups that are not yet generating significant customer adoption or revenue.“[41] This is again why some of the Angel investors and Venture capitalists say that the best time to ask for money is when you do not need it.

Imagine pitching to the investor like a job interview. You will be getting some similar questions. For example, what makes you the right person to run this organisation. The correct answer is usually something along the lines of „Well, I have been working hard and brought us this far. Even though I may lack some experience I am willing to work together with people who do have it and if necessary I would step down to protect the interest of the company“. Always be confident and have a 'but statement' which will say that you are not so full of yourself and that you would rather step down than see the company go down.

Modern *crowdfunding* is a relatively new way of funding your campaigns, but it originated much earlier. First crowdfunding reaches as far as 1700's when the author Jonathan Swift founded Irish Loan Fund. In 1800's this type of funding was used by as many as 20% of households. Dr. Mohammad Yunus is the person that is atributed with founding modern microfinancing, for which he received a

---

[40] C. Freeburn, How to Get Money to Start a Business – 8 Startup Financin Options, Money Crashers, http://www.moneycrashers.com/money-start-small-business-financing-options/ [Accessed: 24.09.2017.]
[41] B. Schroeder, Fail Fast or Win Big, AMACOM, 2015, p. 106

Nobel prize in 2006. Crowdfunding shouldn't be confused with crowdsourcing, which is actually a focus group of people who are working on making certain products better.

Crowdfunding is especially good in this line of business when you need to pay for the order before you can try to sell it. This way you will basically be doing marketing and taking pre-orders. If you are interested in some of the legalities of Crowdfunding in the USA, you could check out the JOBS Act. No, this has nothing to do with Steve Jobs, it stands for Jumpstart Our Business Startups.

This will be marketed to you as a free effort, but it has some hidden costs. Once you create your free account and start your free campaign and start marketing it, you will get loads of requests from certain people and companies to help you with your marketing and targeted audience for a fee. Also, those crowdfunding sites will take a certain percentage from the money you raise and it will depend how much they take from the type of campaign you have chosen. Some websites also have an 'administration fee' or whatever they choose to call it, which they charge to successful fundraisers. Some charge a percentage both from you and your investors. GoFundMe claims not to take any money from your investor's side.

You will need a nice, almost professional video, to engage your backers – 50% of the projects with a video get funded, while only 30% of the projects without one get funded. The video should be 2-3 minutes long. This short format will also make you use a principle which is good not only for crowdfunding, but also in business in general, which is MED – Minimum Effective Dose. MED is the smallest input needed to achieve the desired effect. This is not only good for keeping some of your secrets, but you also do not want to overwhelm you potential backers with information they do not need. Apart from the introduction video, you could also consider making a „milestone video", so if you get to 50% funding you could send an e-mail to your backers that you are „halfway there" and to encourage them to share the campaign and promote it a little bit more. There is another important reason why you want to get beyond those 50% and that is because most of the crowdfunding capaigns that have failed have done so in the 10-50% range, so that is considered a „danger zone". Also, it is a higher possibility that your campaign will get funded if you provide some information about yourself too. Truthfull information. Not too much, but not too few either. Age, name and picture will be enough.

Another good practice is to have a launch day. There are two major reasons for this. One is that you want it to push you and give you a deadline, so you are more productive and the other is that you do not want to have your release date coincide with a release date of some other major company or anything that may distract people from your campaign.

It is also good practice to start promoting the campaign some time earlier, before its start, you may boost those social media posts for instance. But sharing it once a day won't be enough. Create a Facebook group for your early backers, create a Facebook event for when you will be launching your crowdfunding campaign. Now, I wouldn't advise this usually because you wouldn't want people to get the idea that you are postponing something because there's some issues or something else, but changing the time on an event will also send the people who are already following it a notification to remind them of it and that there is now a new time frame. It's a nice trick, but don't do it too often. You do not want to spam the people following you and have them opt out of it. Another nice way of promoting your campaign is creating thousands of free ambassadors for yourself. Create a picture frame that people can insert their photo in and use it on Facebook. If you create it for different amounts of pledges, even better.

Accept this as your real job for the time being at least. Crowdfunding campaigns don't last forever, so it is good to have people interested in funding your cause already lined up. Also, always keep in mind that you do not want to set a goal for the exact number you need. As much as you want to be realistic, some of that money may get lost in the process (administration fees, money transfers, dropped backers, shipping costs for rewards and tax in your country), so add at least 20% more on top of what you really need and hope you get even more. If you are that lucky to get funded, you should always have plans for what if it gets „overfunded". This is where you have stretch goals and if it gets a certain amount of funding you may be adding more products, improving the existing one or something similar. But be mindful. It is much better to get overfunded than to not achieve a goal. So, set your goal carefully and modestly, asking for enough to do what you want.

Plan ahead. If your product is good and you do a great job in preparing for the campaign, especially if it takes of the very first day, then the press may very well be interested in you and will start covering your story. And once this attention subsides, you may be contacting them anyway. So, instead of answering all the same e-mails to everyone who wants to do an article on you, prepare a press kit. A story about your company, how did you come up with the idea, what you want to solve, a few pictures they can use, maybe a promotional video, etc.

There are several types of crowdfunding. Not all might be available to you on every crowdfunding site, but it is good to know there are options out there. Some people consider peer to peer lending and profit sharing (pledging earnings) also crowdfunding, but we'll talk about those later on in this section. The other types are: Reward-based crowdfunding, equity crowdfunding, donation-based crowdfunding and hybrid models.

Reward-based crowdfunding means that you will be rewarding your pledgers with whatever you have promised them for the ammount of money they pledged to you. *Equity crowdfunding* is almost like the regular sale of stocks, you're just selling the stake in your company in a different market. Equity crowdfunding is receiving attention from policymakers as a potential source of funds for start-ups, a segment of the economy that has limited access to finance. Young firms have no track record and often lack assets to be used as guarantees for bank loans. With *donation-based crowdfunding* you usually do not offer rewards, since it's done for charity. *Hybrid models* will allow you to combine more models into one anyway it suits you and what the crowdfunding site is offering you.

A variation of reward based crowdfunding you could try out is a lottery. You are basically running a reward-based crowdfunding campaign, but people pledging to the campaign are only buying a lottery ticket and aren't guaranteed a reward. It would most likely be a bad idea to only have this as your incentive, but it is a nice idea for a cheaper kind of pledge for the wider audience that will not cost you a massive amount of money on sending the rewards out.

Personally, I'd avoid equity crowdfunding, since you may find yourself in an unfavourable position and have someone ask for more than they would realistically get. You need to protect the equity as much as you can, so you later have more „leverage" for future investors, partners, employees, etc. „For example, some investors may ask for board seats. Unless the investor is hugely strategic or invests more than 50 percent of your target amount, think long and hard about such requests."[42] But if you do want to check some of the options for this, then you could check out the next platforms:
1. Micro Ventures
2. Our Crowd
3. Grow Venture Community
4. Circle Up

---

[42] B. Schroeder, Fail Fast or Win Big, AMACOM, 2015, p. 116

5. Crowdfunder

And don't be afraid that your project isn't worthy of it. There have been crowdfunding campaigns for movies, music albums, humanitarian crowdfundings, new businesses, even buying yourself something for birthday or starting a YouTube channel etc. And recently it has gotten so far that people are crowdfunding campaigns to prove if the Earth is flat or not.[43]

You could choose to get the money only if you reach the ammount you need. If you do not reach it, the money goes back to your funders. No harm, no foul. But some sites will offer you a type of campaign where you will be able to keep the money even if you do not reach your set goal, but then you will be obliged to deliver and you will need to honor your promises to your backers. By promises I mean the rewards you can offer to people who fund your campaign. If you're writing a book and promisse to send a book to a backer who donates X ammount of money, then you may need to send it even if you didn't reach your goal. You will need to control yourself here. Do not try to please everyone and make rewards for everyone. Instead of 25, have a maximum of 10 or less.

For the crowdfunding platforms in the UK, you can visit CrowdingIn. These are some of the popular crowdfunding websites:
1. GoFundMe
2. Indiegogo
3. Kickstarter
4. EquityNet
5. SeedUps
6. Peerbackers
7. RocketHub
8. SeedInvest
9. Seedrs (UK and wider Europe)
10. Crowdfunding International (EU)
11. Ketto (India/Asia)
12. Fuel A Dream (India)
13. My Cause (Australia)

Even Facebook is trying out some funding options. I believe this has started with creating campaigns for your birthday, so instead of receiving a present you

---

[43] C. Bell, Rapper B.o.B. raising funds to check if Earth is flat, BBC News, http://www.bbc.com/news/blogs-trending-41399164 [Accessed: 26.09.2017.]

ask your friends to send some money for some cause of your choosing. Now it has grown to a smaller crowdfunding network. Facebook says they do not charge anything for a humanitarian cause, but will charge something for personal funds.

Apart from these websites, there are also some of the more specialized crowdfunding platforms, such as Teespring, which is crowdfunding for T-Shirts. Patreon, on the other hand, will allow you to be a content creator of any kind and have people choose a monthly recurring "membership fee".

There certainly are advantages to crowdfunding, one of which is actually testing your market and impact, but there are also downsides to it which you need to be aware of. The most obvious one is that there are no guarantees that you will get the money. But that one becomes even worse combined with the risk you may take once your idea goes public and you can't continue pursuing it for the time being. You could be underestimating the cost. You may not just be missing the hidden costs of this business, but also the provision that the crowdfunding site will take and all the other transaction costs. Since crowdfunding is still relatively new, you should try to get all the information you can on the law around it, so you don't accidentaly break it. There is always a risk of people trying to get easy money, so they create fraudulent platforms. So always check the platform you will be working with and do your due dilligence.

If you are from a country that is in the European Union you can find some information about the crowdfunding and many other topics on the website of European Comission, like the following regulations. Given the great variety of crowdfunding campaigns, different EU rules might apply to crowdfunding, depending on the features of the specific campaign. The Anti-Money Laundering Directive and the Regulation on information on the payer accompanying transfers of funds aim at preventing money laundering and apply to crowdfunding under the same conditions as for any other type of financial transaction. The Regulations on unitary patent protection aim at creating a more easily accessible patent across EU countries for those project owners who wish to protect their invention before disclosing it to the public. The E-commerce Directive facilitates market access across the EU for platforms and lays down liability rules of on-line intermediaries. The Directive on misleading and comparative advertising and the Directive on unfair commercial practices aim to protect consumers and ensure fair advertising practices. Further EU rules may apply to financial-return forms of crowdfunding, depending on the type of activity and the specific business model used. These include the Prospectus Directive, the Payment Services Directive, MiFID, CRD IV, AIFMD, the Consumer Credit Directive, the Distance Marketing of Financial

Services and the Regulations on Capital Requirements, European Venture Capital and European Social Entrepreneurship Funds.[44]

Industry estimates show that almost half a million projects were financed through crowdfunding across Europe during 2012, raising €735 million, 65% more than in 2011. Total Global Crowdfunding Industry estimated fundraising volume in 2015 was $34 Billion. By region this means that North America gave $17.2 Billion, Asia $10.54 Billion, Europe $6.48 Billion, Oceania $68.6 Million, South America $85.74 Million, Africa $24.16 Million.[45]

Angel investor is a term I only heard about when I started to think about how I would finance my line of products. These are people who are often very established in investing into start-ups and they tend to keep to their own niche. So, someone who is used to investing in an automotive industry most likely won't invest in cosmetics. I wouldn't expect Mark Cuban to jump on board even if I suggested the Mavericks shower gel. But still, this is a very important part of funding as banks can be very reluctant to give money to anyone who is new in the business and doesn't really have a track record to show for.

Angel investors don't only offer financing to start up your business, some are willing to provide guidance based on their own experience. They can also use their existing contacts within an industry to open doors for your business. So, how do you find these angel investors? It can take some research since "many angel investors prefer to keep a low profile and can only be identified by asking other business owners or financial advisors. Other angels have joined networks, making it easier for potential startups to locate them."[46] Here are a number of organizations that can put your business in contact with angel investors, both individually and in groups:
1. Go4Funding
2. Tech Coast Angels
3. Investors' Circle
4. Golden Seeds LLC
5. Band of Angels

---

[44] Communication on crowdfunding in the Europen Union – Frequently Asked Questions, European Commission, http://europa.eu/rapid/press-release_MEMO-14-240_en.pdf [Accessed: 24.09.2017.]
[45] Crowdfunding Industry Report, Crowdexpert, http://crowdexpert.com/crowdfunding-industry-statistics/, [Accessed: 24.09.2017.]
[46] C. Freeburn, How to Get Money to Start a Business – 8 Startup Financin Options, Money Crashers, http://www.moneycrashers.com/money-start-small-business-financing-options/ [Accessed: 24.09.2017.]

6. Hyde Park Angels
7. Alliance of Angels
8. AngelList
9. Angel Capital Association

In his book *"Fail Fast or Win Big"* author Bernhard Schröder notes that „Angel investors typically only do one to three deals per year and average in the $25,000 to $100,000 range. Through their formal and informal networks, angel investors might be exposed to 15 to 20 companies per month."[47] So the odds of grabbing an angel investor's attention aren't especially high, but they're still better than the chances of getting a venture capital firm to invest in your startup business.

You may get a 'No' for an answer from an Angel investor. But 'no' doesn't always mean 'no'. *(Please don't take this as dating advice).* If they do not invest now in you, it doesn't mean that they do not like the idea and that they might not want to invest in you in the future. It just may not be the right time for your startup. Maybe it's too soon for your product for the market (it's certainly a more optimistic way of looking at it, rather than being too late), maybe it's some other issue. The first electric car isn't a Tesla or Rimac, it's Riker from 1898.

When is the best time to ask for money? Usually it's when you already have money. Angel investors will go on board with someone who is partially funded and who already has skin in the game. They will, on the other hand, rarely invest only in your idea, without a company, without anything. It's also good to have a product to show or some kind of prototype of it. In cosmetics business this becomes harder because to get to the product stage you will have to invest a lot of money and if you get there you really shouldn't need that much more money.

Mark Cuban often says that the best kind of equity is ***sweat equity.*** This basically means you have started from something smaller and then continued to work and develop and grow. This is what the investors would appreciate too. They do not want to see that the only skill you have is raising funds. And in Mark's eyes the first time you have failed is when you took money from someone, because you couldn't get it organically.

Other platforms are also emerging in the era of entrepreneurship and startups. There are various companies that would provide you with some sort of assistance in the endevour of launching your business. Startups.co is a website

---

[47] B. Schroeder, Fail Fast or Win Big, AMACOM, 2015, p. 106

which is a family of six products, as they describe themselves. *Startups.co* provides education, *bizplan* provides planning, *clarity* will provide mentors, *fundable* will help you with funding, *launchrock* will help with customers and *zirtual* will help as a virtual assistant. A similar website that helps you with your startup is Gust.

You could also **try to pledge some of your future earnings** through an online marketplace called the Thrust Fund. You would offer a percentage of your future lifetime earnings in exchange for upfront, undesignated venture funding. Beware: the legality and enforceability of these „personal investment contracts" have yet to be established.

Factoring is a finance method where a company sells its receivables at a discount price to get cash upfront. It's often used by companies with poor credit or by businesses such as apparel manufacturers, which have to fill orders long before they get paid. However, this is an expensive way to raise funds. Companies selling receivables generally pay a percentage of the total amount. If you pay a 2 percent fee to get funds 30 days in advance, it's equivalent to an annual interest rate of about 24 percent. For that reason, the business has gotten a bad reputation over the years.

Peer-to-peer lending (sometimes called crowdlending, also debt-based crowdfunding) means borrowing money without going through a traditional bank or investment company. „Under P2P a borrower posts a loan request on a P2P platform – such as Lending Club or Prosper – stating the amount desired and reason for the loan. Potential investors review the request and agree to loan various amounts of money to the borrower up to the desired amount."[48] This can be done also vice versa and lenders can bid on the loan by offering better interest rates. Once a loan has been funded, the borrower receives the total amount lent and then pays the loan back through fixed monthly payments made to the platform, which then repays the investors based on the amount each one lent.

Some of the platforms to look at are:
1. Lending Club
2. Prosper
3. Funding Circle
4. Index Ventures

---

[48] C. Freeburn, How to Get Money to Start a Business – 8 Startup Financing Options, Money Crashers, http://www.moneycrashers.com/money-start-small-business-financing-options/ [Accessed: 24.09.2017.]

5. Zidisha
6. Quarter Spot
7. Fundation
8. Kiva
9. Assetz Capital (UK)
10. Zopa (UK)

Accelerators are also a possibility. The way an accelerator works is that, depending on the size of an accelerator, the applicants may go through three stages. In the first stage they would have the largest number of applicants in and they would give them a chance to work on their ideas. At the first stage, at the HUB, an idea is all you need and you will spend 30-45 days working on it. In the accelarator phase you will need to have a company and more than just an idea and in this phase there are fewer people than in the first one. After the accelerator comes the first pitch to the investors and you may get sent back to work more on the idea and try later or you may get sent to a larger accelerator and even end up in silicone valley. Accelerators are often focused on the IT sector, but some of the other ideas can sneak in also. Accelerators will usually take 8%, 4% and another 4% through the three stages of this process.

Incubators are something that often gets confused with accelerators. To put it simply, if accelerators are places to work on your idea and your start-up and maybe fine-tune it a little, incubators are places to work on your company. Most of the things that end up in the incubator are high quality ideas and companies so the process of getting into an incubator isn't short or easy. Incubators can also be focused on certain areas. If one is sponsored by a hospital, then that particular incubator may be looking for technologies in the area of healthcare.

The good thing with both, accelerators and incubators, is that they often also provide you with a space to work from and exposure through their networks. Not to mention the mentors who will work with you and help you through some of the issues you may face.

Apply to visit a TV show like Shark Tank in the USA or Dragons Den in the UK. Here entrepreneurs apply to pitch Sharks/Dragons such as Mark Cuban, Barbara Corcoran, Robert Hernjavec and others. There is really not much to say about this if you've already seen at least one episode. Basically, entrepreneurs are getting a chance to pitch their idea to the investors on the show and if they like it, they will make you an offer. This offer goes with some conditions, usually it's a part of your company, they may ask you to have a higher price on your product so they can get more money faster or to have more say in your company than you may like with bringing in other investors or using you to advertise something you may or may not like, etc. Apart from being able to pitch your idea to people who have vast amounts of experience in starting and running companies, you are also getting a huge amount of free PR. By appearing on this show, you are also appearing on peoples TV screens in prime time, probably YouTube, etc. If you haven't already made sure that your website hosting service/package can handle all the traffic, it might be good to do. So maybe the PR isn't free, but the PR is very often even a larger reason people visit these shows and not the sharks.

VC, Angel Investors, Sharks, etc… Any kind of investors will be interested not necessarily in your product, but in your business. Especially if you have anticipated and solved ahead of time any issues you may face. They are more interested whether or not someone else will buy your product, not how you'll make them want it. Talking to an investor is not the same as talking to a consumer. Consumer falls in love with a product, an investor falls in love with the business, the idea execution, how well you know the market and how you would solve any challenges you more than likely will face.

This last one doesn't have much to do with starting up a business and this too is the first time I am hearing about this type of funding. And even though it doesn't apply to funding a business directly, it may be applied indirectly. Personally, I hope you never need to use it. This is ***litigation crowdfunding***. "Litigation crowdfunding allows plaintiffs or defendants to reach out to hundreds of their peers simultaneously in a semiprivate and confidential manner to obtain funding, either seeking donations or providing a reward in return for funding. It also allows investors to purchase a stake in a claim they have funded, which may allow them to get back more than their investment if the case succeeds (the reward is based on the compensation received by the litigant at the end of his or her case, known as a contingent fee in the United States, a success fee in the United Kingdom, or a *pactum de quota litis* in many civil law systems)."[49] A platform that allows accredited investors to invest in lawsuits is LexShares.

4.3 Do you need all that money

I started out with an idea of around 25 cosmetic products and some additional complimentary products that would go with those. Only for R&D I

---

[49]   Crowdfunding,   Wikipedia,   https://en.wikipedia.org/wiki/Crowdfunding,   [Accessed: 24.09.2017.]

would have needed around 70,000 USD. This is an estimated price based on the two products I have received an invoice for. Some of the other products would have been simpler, which would also lower the price a little, but that doesn't matter.

What matters is do you need those 25 products to make your offer complete? Some people will recommend you only start with one product. And I am against that if you believe that you cannot do that and that you want to provide more than just a soap, maybe you want to provide a complete feeling of cleanliness and even some sort of accomplishment that isn't possible with a simple soap.

But you may not need 25 products for that either. I thought my idea is the best idea and it needs to have 25 products to blow everyone away, but you could actually start with only 7 products and still cover everything. I am not saying to give up on the 25, but to start a line a smaller number is enough. Knowing this will help you reach that crowdfunding goal or sell the number to someone else just a little bit better in case they can't swallow the higher one.

4.4 Pitching

We have mentioned pitching a few times by now, but never really explained how to do this. Well, there are certainly more ways to do this, but we'll address only two.

First of all, it would be nice for you to know what an *elevator pitch* is. This is basically a pitch that you can deliver to a person of interest while sharing an elevator with him or her – around 30 seconds. Now, I encourage you to have one, I encourage you to practice one and I encourage you not to use one.

Why do I say this? Because, I believe that your elevator pitch should be a practice for you to be able to explain your company in the first minute of your pitch and that everybody should be able to understand you. That is all an elevator pitch should be, something to get you through the door. I have yet to hear that a contract has been signed based on a blitz elevator pitch. It is more likely that you will be invited to a meeting and asked to do a real pitch.

Meetings are usually scheduled for an hour, but you should keep your pitch much shorter, 20-30 minutes, ideally 20. You will want to account for somebody being late or a previous meeting lasting longer and you will want to incorporate Q&A into your pitch. The pitch should also be accompanied by data, the data would be made in form of a presentation. Guy Kawasaki suggests following a 10/20/30 rule – 10 slides, 20 minutes, 30 pt font.

The presentation should also be *fluid*. This means that the transitions from topic to topic or slide to slide need to make sense. This will also help you to give a better oral presentation and without weird transitions. The presentation needs to be *readable*. We go back to the rule about the font in a sense. If you know how large the room will be, you should take care that the person in the last row can read it easily. Use *as few words as possible*. Steve Jobs and some other entrepreneurs could use even one or two words. Seth Godin recommends that you use maximum of six words. You should be able to *refer* to your slides – they should back your speech, people should not be able to read what you are saying.

Some think that all the bullet points should appear at once, instead one by one. I am not sure if I would agree with this. Actually, on the one hand I will agree with this if the bullets are only a list you go through at once, on the other hand if you will stay at each bullet and say something, I would say have them appear one by one in order to prevent people going too far ahead.

There is also some etiquette to making PowerPoint presentations for a business. Do not use flashy backgrounds and do not use different backgrounds for every slide. You want a dark background. Navy blue is always a nice colour for a background and for a suit. All pages should have your logo, do not use **Comic Sans** fonts, Arial or Times New Roman is great. Actually, sans serif fonts (Arial, Helvetica, Myriad Pro, **Verdana**) are often used for titles and serif fonts (Times New Roman, Garamond, Goudy, Palatino) for the body of the presentation. Do not use 45 animations for your slides, actually don't use any and don't use sounds unless you really need to.

You can print the presentation out and use it as your material for the meeting, but I think that you should spend some more time and write it in Word, where you will use footnotes for every more important fact. PowerPoint sadly still didn't come that far to look good when printed out (often it even looks bad on the screen) and a printed out presentation can leave an impression of laziness. You could also add into this document many things that couldn't fit into your presentation and when presenting you could just say to the people following you what page to open.

No matter what Guy or I think about the time you have for your pitch/presentation, always check with the people you are pitching. Be respectful of their time and always ask how much of it you may have. It is not enough only to ask this. Also keep to that time. You should also know what are the most important things they want you to present, if you will be going through the presentation and then taking questions or will you be taking questions after each segment, do they have a projector, if they don't do they mind if you bring yours, etc. If it's possible and the meeting room isn't occupied can you get there 15 minutes before and set up your laptop and prepare the presentation.

Who is the person delivering the pitch? Ideally, that would be the CEO of the company and not the whole team. This is a company you are most likely leading, it's not a 60's band sharing one microphone on the stage. I have repeated that this is also a reason the CEO had good communication skills. The reason for this is that you do not want to have a bad presentation because the people listening to it notice if someone didn't prepare for it and if someone who isn't supposed to really work closely with people doesn't have the skills to get the needed message across. This may lead to people not really understanding some parts of the presentation clearly and you not landing the deal you needed. The only reason why you should bring someone along is if the presentation calls for some piece of information that is too technical and you do not understand everything in detail to be able to speak about it with full confidence.

After the pitch is done you will likely be sitting down for a conversation. You will still need to show your smarts. This time it won't be with information, it's with paying attention, not interrupting them mid-sentence and taking notes of their questions, concerns and reminders with which you will want to answer said questions and concerns.

5 The prospect of being rich

This book would have probably sold much better if it had some keywords in the title, like 'rich', 'millionaire', 'billionaire' and variations on that topic. The reasons why those books sell that good is because people want to get rich fast and easy. I have a solution for you. Buy a lottery ticket and pray to whatever God you believe in that you win.

But if you actually want to take your financial status into your own hands instead of hoping that you will be one out of who knows how many people who bought a lottery ticket, then it would be a good idea to finish reading this book, learn a few more things from it, write your statement of what you want to do and how you plan to achieve it and by when. Read another book if you need to, although I don't suggest looking for more information about starting a cosmetic line, I think you're at the right spot here. If you need to, read this one again, but then start doing something. No amount of reading will get the ball rolling, only you getting out there and taking a chance on some things will.

Everybody at least once in their lifetime says they want to be rich and financially free and secure, but they only see the tip of the iceberg. They come closer and suddenly when they see the full size of it, it's not so appealing anymore – the work, the sacrifice that goes into it doesn't look so good.

5.1 How to get rich

There are many people out there who will want to sell you the secret to how to get rich. There are many videos on YouTube that will tell you how to earn money online. Strangely, every video about how to make money online makes all its money teaching you how to make money or it ends up being a bait to a seminar someone will try to sell you.

It's pretty much the same with people who will try to teach you about assets and how to get those. But those are big investments and if you're searching on the internet how to get rich or earn money online, you probably don't have the kind of money to buy a house or a flat and start renting it. But it's the time of Airbnb, start with a room maybe and go bigger.

It seems like only one statement is true here... If you want to get rich, write a book about how to get rich. Anything with 'rich' or 'millionaire' in the title is destined to sell well because people don't know how to do it. It certainly isn't impossible and there are people out there who have some smart things to say, but do not fall for every quick money video or advice you get across.

For money to start flowing, you will need to start attracting money, as Napoleon Hill put it. Attracting money means having the mindset that you want to have money and be rich. But do not stop with wanting 'a lot'. Define the amount and go for it. Start working for that money. And I don't mean a job, but working nonetheless. Surfing the Facebook on your phone and hoping money materialises in front of you will not cut it.

So if you are reading this book and thinking about starting your own cosmetic line or some other business, then I would say you are on the right track. Keep working, keep trying and keep reading books like this. And there is no way you can escape reading books today. You can buy various kinds of books, be it paperback or hardcover, e-books could be cheaper and they don't take up any space. Even dyslexia isn't an excuse anymore. You could listen to an audiobook at your home or every time you are in your car driving to and from your work. The thing you start with is yourself. Start with the man in the mirror. Invest in yourself, develop yourself and then you will be able to develop your company and your products.

There is only one thing you need to know and make your peace with – THERE ARE NO SHORTCUTS. The people writing the books, the YouTubers, the whatevers have not become rich overnight. People have been posting videos for a long time to get to several million subscribers. There is this „measure" of some kind that it takes you at least 10 years to become a professional and in case of photography it is said that you need 10,000 photographs. People sometimes talk about an anecdote about Debbie Millman when she designed a logo for one company and charged some large amount of money. Someone complained that it has taken her only two minutes and she replied, „2 minutes and 34 years". Similar anecdote, as told by Austin Kleon, follows Pablo Picasso. A lady wanted a portrait of her dog in the park and he does something in his style and very quickly and asks 5,000 USD and the lady complains that it has taken him only a few seconds and Picasso replies, „Madam, it has taken me my whole life".

As Robert Kiyosaki's rich dad put it, "Keep working boys, but the sooner you forget about needing a paycheck, the easier your adult life will be. Keep using your brain, work for free, and soon your mind will show you ways of making money far beyond what I could ever pay you. You will see things that other people never see. Most people never see these opportunities because they're looking for money and security, so that's all they get. The moment you see one opportunity, you'll see them for the rest of your life". This is why I suggest you go back to the start and read again the part about passion. You need to put effort in what you are doing, not just be passionate about it.

And please do not listen to anyone who tells you that to become rich you should stop drinking coffee or something like that. You do not get rich by saving money on coffee, the coffee you may drink with someone may actually be the reason for your wealth. Which brings us to a different point, *do still drink coffee or your beverage of choice, but choose the people you do that with*. You are the average of the five people you spend the most time with.

One more very important thing. Do not go ahead and look at what rich people are doing now. Comparing yourself to some of the richest and most powerful people now can even be demoralising and depressing. If you want to try and replicate the result of now rich people, you should go ahead and see what they were doing BEFORE they were rich. They started out of garages, sleeping in offices, getting creative even with where they would take a shower. You won't start with an office building in your name, but you need to start. Being an entrepreneur in the past used to be an euphemism that you had no job and were a failure, now it's regarded and romanticized as something everybody strives for. If you want to look at someone, maybe also go look at people who have failed. Learning from them may be as important, if not more. "If you undertake this job, you should interview not only the few who have succeeded, but the many who have failed. You should carefully analyze many thousands of people who have been classed as 'failures', and I mean by the term 'failures', men and women who come to the closing chapter of life disappointed because they did not attain the goal which they had set their hearts upon achieving. As inconsistent as it may seem, you will learn more about how to succeed from the failures than you will from the so-called successes. They will teach you what not to do."[50]

5.2 How to stay rich

If, or, if you keep developing yourself through this and other books, rather when you get rich… How do you stay that way? It doesn't matter how much you make, it's more important how much you keep. "Money without financial

---

[50] N. Hill, Outwitting the Devil, Sterling, New York, 2013, p. 4

intelligence is money soon gone."[51] And one of the first ways that you will show your financial literacy is by showing you understand what the rich people do, the difference between assets and liabilities.

We spoke about habits earlier. Well, rich people tend to have one more. They do not spend all their money on phones, cars and golden toilet seats. These are liabilities. Everything that takes money, instead of pays, is a liability. So, if you want to save some money, these are just three examples. Home is also a liability, because it only costs you money, but another apartment that you rent isn't. Stocks and royalties from intellectual property are also assets. And Robert Kiyosaki's rich dad suggests that you only buy the things you love, because that way you'll show more interest in them and in case any issues arise you'll have an easier time dealing with those.

Rich people do not spend, they invest. Or as Robert Kiyosaki put it, "The poor and middle class work for money. Rich have money work for them." I mentioned earlier that if you are surfing the internet for ways to earn money, you probably don't have means to buy a house or an apartment to rent those. But real estate isn't only buildings, that can also be just a vacant land. If you purchase "regular" land and if you are able to get an industrial license for it with all the other paperwork, you have just made it more profitable without doing anything on it. This kind of land can become attractive to the city or some company.

This is what they call passive income.

Rich people also know what is important for them to stay rich. They are. They will keep investing in knowledge, learning their whole life, following new trends and technologies, keeping their mind fresh and active.

To shorten this a little… Whenever you use a word 'spend', that is probably what rich people are not doing or doing less or smarter. Whenever you use the word 'invest', that is where they excel. You spend money on clothes, cars, phones, gadgets. You invest in yourself (knowledge), businesses, stocks, property.

This isn't to say that you shouldn't have any nice things, you certainly shouldn't be working in some rugged clothes and go to meetings looking like a cave man, this is to remind you to set your priorities and that when you're running

---

[51] R. Kiyosaki, Rich dad, poor dad, Time Warner Books UK, 2007

your business your first priority is keeping the doors open, paying bills and getting yours and everyone else's paycheck on time. Everything else is a luxury.

5.3 Learn from Rotary

If you have a pulse, by now you should have heard about Rotary International and Rotary Clubs in the world. Rotary International has adopted a test in the 1940's that is now known as the four-way test, which many people and clubs have written about.[52]

The four-way test was created in 1932 by its author Herbert J. Taylor. Herbert was tasked to save Club Aluminum Company from being closed as a bankrupt organization. The company owed 400.000 USD, but was somehow still alive. Herbert even invested 6.100 USD of his own money just to have something to operate with.

Since the competitors of the company had equal quality products, they were aware that this is not something they could be working on at this point. So, they decided that it should be the character and dependability that will set the bar higher and distinguish them from their competition. They have become more careful in selecting their personnel and were also helping the ones they had to become better men and women.

Many industries had a code of ethics and that is how the four-way test has started, as a 100-word statement. But codes were hard to remember. Codes were also stating what someone should be doing and Herbert didn't want them to be imperative. So the code became seven questions, only to reach its ultimate form of four questions in 24 words. The goal was to ask questions which, when asked, would help a person find out whether the *"things we think, say or do"* were right or wrong. These are the four questions:

1. Is it the truth?
2. Is it fair to all concerned?
3. Will it build good will and better friendships?
4. Will it be beneficial to all concerned?

---

[52] The information about the four-way test we have here was from two websites - http://thefourwaytest.com/history-of-the-four-way-test/ and http://www.rotary5630.org/history-of-the-four-way-test/ [Accessed: 18.11.2017.]

The first person to try the test out was Herbert. After two months he had brought his four department heads to ask them what they thought of it. Eventually, the whole company started using the test and everyone was asked to memorize it. The test was used in business when making decisions, it was used to make revised statements about their products, not using any superlative words or statements they could not prove. Even all negative language about competitors products was removed from their literature. Not only that, but even when they could speak well of their competitors, they did that. But it was also used in private lives.

The orders started coming in. One day an order of 50.000 utensils was announced. They all needed a sale that large, but the sales manager found out that the potential customer intended to sell the products at cut-rate prices. Putting that through the 4-way test, the sales manager decided that it wouldn't be fair to their regular dealers who were promoting their product consistently. By saying 'no' to some clients they were even losing money, but by 1937 the debt the company had was paid off. From a company that was bankrupt in 1932, they had paid off their debts and paid its stockholders over one million in dividends over the next 15 years. Its net worth climbed to over two million.

We live in a real and rough world, that's a given. So if you try and apply this 4-way test to your business and life and sometimes you feel you cannot apply it, then don't. But don't give up on the test. This is not some dogma, some doctrine you need to live by. You will not be failing Herbert, the Rotary organization or yourself. By even trying, and doing it as much as you can, applying the 4-way test in business will ultimately be shaping you as a person, helping you to be better. Not just a better businessman, but a better partner, a better parent, whatever you choose. Once you start applying the test, it is hard to turn it off outside of work, because it becomes a part of you.

I also encourage you to use the experience of Rotary when creating your own operations manual. At first, this is good to have for yourself, to be reminded of your goals and missions and how you wish to achieve those. But as your company grows, you will not be able to oversee everything, so it's good to have something your employees can fall back on when they need some reference or what you can use if you ever need to have a talk with them for not doing something as described. This also means that once created, the manual may not be shelved and forgotten, it needs to be reinforced into the consciousness of everyone who is involved in the company.

Every manual is different and you can make one for each department – President, Marketing, HR – and you can make one for employees including everything up to the dress code, should you wish to go in that much detail. If you were running a coffee shop, you'd write here that the waiter has to give the guests time to sit down and make themselves comfortable before he ambushes them with an order. This will be good for your new employees and may make their settling in the company easier. It can be good and attractive to clients too.

But most of all, I encourage you to use the 4-way test because, like I said, it is not only business related and it doesn't only help us build a good business, but good and honest relationships in and outside of business.

5.4 Define what success means to you

I am putting this part of the book here because for many people success means making insane amounts of money. And it certainly doesn't hurt to have that money. But if you determine what success means early on, you may be a lot happier.

Many people believe that success is when you are working less and earning more. So they start looking for a way to achieve this, hence the success of Tim's book „*The 4-hour workweek*". This doesn't have to be true. Maybe you fall into the group of people who like to work. Maybe you enjoy working and being occupied by something. The secret to happiness, at least in regards to work, is not working less. The secret is finding the work you love. „Personally, I like work. I believe in a 168-hour workweek that is filled with the activities I love. A few hours of sleep can be thrown in if necessary."[53]

There is also nothing wrong if you define success as having 250,000 USD in sales. That's not a bad measure of it. But is that what you want? Is that what you need? Maybe your lifestyle doesn't really require that much money. Maybe you are a more modest person. Maybe success to you is to have the doors of your company open and to have just enough money to be comfortable and safe, so that you do not worry if your family has enough, are the bills paid and is there food on the table.

Once you define success like this it won't matter if the sales are lower if you're managing to do all this. Sales may get higher eventually, but you setting a

---

[53] C. Guillebeau, The Art of non-conformity, Tarcher Perigee, 2010., p 102

measure of success for yourself will save you from a lot of stress if you compare yourself to someone else. There will always be someone else who earns more. And it is dangerous to compare your behind the scenes to someone else's highlight reel. I already mentioned what Elon Musk has went through in his business and private life, I mentioned what his friend said about running a business, other people who have struggled starting a business from cheap locations, like Bill Gates and Mark Cuban. Those people are a great success today, but in order to deal with your ups and downs better you also need to know that the people you are comparing yourself to also had those issues at some point in their lives. Also, it may be better if you compare yourself to who you were yesterday, not who someone else is today. „Finally, you might come to realize that the specifics of the many games you are playing are so unique to you, so individual, that comparison to others is simply inappropriate. Perhaps you are overvaluing what you don't have and undervaluing what you do. There's some real utility in gratitude. It's also good protection against the dangers of victimhood and resentment. Your colleague outperforms you at work. His wife, however, is having an affair, while your marriage is stable and happy. Who has it better?"[54]

But back to success…

I forget who said this, but it is a story about a fisherman. A fisherman was fishing for a while in his small boat, which caught an eye of some person sitting on the beach. He saw the fisherman caught a few big fish and he was curious, so he asks him: „How long did it take you to catch those fish?" – „Oh, not very long." – „So why don't you stay a little bit longer and catch some more", the person asks – „Well, this is enough to feed my whole family." – „So what do you do for the rest of the day?" – „After fishing I go and play a little with my children, I rest and have a drink with my friends in the evening". Now this person introduces himself and says that he is a lead management guy for this big company and that he can give him some advice. If he were to spend as much time as possible to catch all the fish he could, he could then buy a larger boat, when he buys a larger boat, he would be able to catch even more fish, so he would be able to then buy more boats and now hire people to fish for him, start a company, sell canned fish, have an office building. „And what would I do after that", asks the fisherman? – „After a while you could have a big house in the city and eventually sell your company" – „And then" – „Well, then you would retire in a small fishing village, have a house on the beach, you could go fishing every morning, play with your children, spend time with your family and friends". The fisherman was puzzled, „Isn't that what I am

---

[54] J. B. Peterson, 12 rules for life, an antidote to chaos, Penguin random house, 2018

now doing?" The morale of the story is very similar to the one where a man goes away from home seeking happiness only to figure out when he comas back not finding anything that it was there all the time, in his modest home with his loved ones. As soon as you figure out what your happiness is, the happier you will be.

6 You're almost there

While reading this book you have covered many issues that you will need to tackle when starting your cosmetic line and a business. You are almost there and I hope that the information I have shared was helpful.

We are now very close to the end of our journey to learn about what it takes to have a successful cosmetics business, or any kind of business for that matter. But there are still three key things we need to cover that I felt would get lost if I put them somewhere with the other issues we have covered. That is why the following topics in this part of the book are equally important: partners, making the first step and secrets.

6.1 Partners

The reason I speak about partners in a separate title and not within the funding part is because they are far more than that. Your name may be later recognized as the one who started this venture, innovated, founded the company, etc. But to bring it where you want it to be, you will need, as Guy Kawasaki puts it, a soul mate.

A partner isn't only a person who will give you money to develop your products and place them on the market. This is someone who you will share the rest of your business life with if all goes well. At least with that company. Effectively, a partnership is almost like a marriage – you both sign a paper and if you have a bad break up, you lose your house. The only thing missing is the rings.

When choosing a partner you need to pay attention to a few things. You want to click with your partner and not just when opening Skype for a video conference. It will be far more pleasant to work with a person you like and can relate to. You will also need to check your partner's background. Trust in any relationship is important, but caution is always advised. Whatever information you can get your hands on is good. You also need someone to share your vision with. If your partner doesn't share the vision of your company and your products, the partnership will fall apart. One of the more famous dodgy partnerships is Jobs and Wozniak. All this to say one thing... Date before you marry a business partner, as someone else put it. „Founders should share a prehistory before they start a company together – otherwise they are just rolling the dice."[55]

But what to look for in a business partner? Yes, you want to share the same passion, motivations, want to work to achieve same goals, etc. But what do you need?! First you will need to look at yourself. Are you a more creative person or analytical? Whatever you are, find your opposite. Because if you are a creative enthusiast who acts on impulse because he had this great idea, you will need someone to keep you grounded and offer a more cautious view of things.

But most importantly, you don't only want a partner on paper. You want a partner with „skin in the game" (especially in skin care) – someone who can win or lose from your endeavour, same as you. This makes both of you want to work hard and be passionate about your company and your product, instead of one person working and the other just having a business card with the name of the company on it.

„You need good people who get along, but you also need a structure to help keep everyone aligned for the long term. To anticipate likely sources of misalignment in any company, it is useful to distinguish between three concepts:
- Ownership: Who legally owns the company's equity?
- Possession: Who actually runs the company on a day-to-day basis?
- Control: Who formally governs the company's affairs?

A typical startup allocates ownership among founders, employees and investors. The managers and employees who operate the company enjoy possession. And a board of directors, usually comprising founders and investors, exercises control."[56]

6.2 1 > 0

I imagine that after reading some of the things in this book and most likely in some other books, some of these things could look intimidating. Sometimes you don't even know what is behind the curtains of what you think you desire. And I didn't even touch on it all. But I hope you don't get discouraged and I hope you keep pushing and follow one thought.

---

[55] P. Thiel, Zero to One, notes on startups, or how to build the future, Penguin Random House, 2014., p. 109
[56] Ibid., p. 110

One is greater than zero.

This is something I picked up while following Gary Vaynerchuk. Simplified into two numbers and one symbol it tells you all you need to know about anything… life, business, love, friendship, whatever you wish to apply it to.

Gary actually uses it in a different way, I just added a little bit more positivity to it. Gary's view isn't necessarily negative, it's painfully real. What Gary says is that it baffles him how many people think they are bigger than they actually are. Everyone is shooting for the best and biggest players in specific industries. People want to meet a specific CEO, become a NY Times #1 best selling author, etc. And one is greater than zero. Being on some talk show that doesn't get recognized in the whole world is better than not being on Oprah.

The smarter and strategic thing to do here would be to go on a local talk show or appear in the local news. Then gradually go on larger shows and news. Same goes for news portals and in which order you send your story to them. Your strategy is to create breadcrumbs that a larger news outlet would be able to follow back and check for its credibility. And when other media is covering it then larger ones can't afford not to. It will eventually come to a point where media will take the news from each other without you sending it to them.

Sadly, people are unwilling to climb the ladder. They would rather jump on the last rung and hope it doesn't break or, more often, hope they don't fall. And they do fall. Not only do they fall, they don't even touch the place where they would like to be. People are unwilling to do the time, but they want to be YouTubers, businessmen, authors, etc. over night. *It takes 10 years to become an overnight success and you need to do your 10.000 hours.* Dedication and patience are the foundation of so many things, not only business. I mentioned this already, so many people complain about their YouTube channel not taking off, photographers complaining about not getting work and their work goes back for maybe a month. People you know as an overnight success are the people you haven't heard of for years while they were shooting local weddings and had 10 subscribers for two years.

And Gary is absolutely right. You cannot jump from not being able to walk in the door to being best friends with 50 CEO's and having Fortune 500 names in your cell phone, you cannot jump from having 100 dollars to having 1.000.000 dollars, etc. You also need to keep the humility and still be approachable and value every view, click, share, read, any kind of exposure you get. Because even if you reach a microscopic fraction of an audience, maybe that audience has that one CEO or someone you have been trying to reach.

Other than that, you also want to push yourself every day and do as much as you can do. Don't skip something because you can't do a certain amount of anything at that moment. You can't run three times a week. Run once. You can't do 10 pushups. Do one. There isn't a person in the world that started lifting some crazy amounts of weight the moment they stepped into the gym or ran a marathon without preparing on smaller tracks. There isn't a person who is a great speaker and speaks to thousands of people who didn't speak to 5 people first. So do that one step.

Do that one push-up, run for 100 meters and then walk back, lift a pink dumbbell. Business and entrepreneurship aren't too different from martial arts. You advance from white belt through various colours all the way to black and then degrees of black. There is no way of getting to black without being yellow first. There is no way you can be number one if you weren't number 63 at some point.

Do that one step. One is greater than zero.

6.3 Protecting your idea

When thinking about our innovative idea we often get scared and tend not to talk to anyone about it and that is fine for a while. But you can not be that careful all the time and you want people starting to learn about you even before you're out on the market. So, what do you do?

One way of protecting yourself is *not telling anyone*. Three men can keep a secret if two of them are dead, someone once said. So… keep quiet. If you talk about your plans too freely, you may be surprised to find out that someone else has beaten you to the goal. Another way is *signing the non-disclosure agreement* with people who you need to tell your trade secrets. This will be with a laboratory and anyone you feel you are giving some valuable information about your business. Be careful here. You can ask for an NDA if someone is getting involved with you, but if you are asking for help with something and asking them to sign something, not only will you not get the help, but also make a long lasting bad impression. Similar to the NDA are two other agreements: non-compete agreement and work for hire agreement. The *non-compete agreement* will be preventing people or companies you hire to help you to start a business that would compete with or threaten your company. *Work for hire agreement* basically means that if you hire someone who comes up with something while working for you, you will be the owner of his or her work. In some countries this has an expiration date and it prevents the person only for a certain amount of time. Later the patent or the idea goes back to the author of it. *You* should also *avoid revealing too* much and be strategic about what you say and to whom. If there is anything you should take out of some spy movies, that's the phrase 'need to know'. This means that if you can do business with as few words and details as possible, do it. This also means that you keep track what information you give, to whom you give it and always give a different piece of information to someone else. This way, even if it leaks, you will know where from. And there's always a possibility of *having trustworthy people* around you, who you know will not share something important to you. But even then... It is in my nature to not give up all the information I have, I am also a little bit paranoid like that. And because of that, you should always do your due diligence and research the people and companies you are working with.

People often mistakenly think that when they have something important to protect, they should patent it. A patent is only serving as a protection of something that is innovative. For something to be protected by a patent it needs to be an innovation, but a patent is only one part of intellectual property rights. And to be fair, patenting something is a double-edged sword. While it could seem like a logical thing to do and something you could eventually profit from in the future (but probably not in this business) you open up yourself to patent trolls. These are basically people who have found it lucrative to sue companies and challenge their patents because most companies did not want to go into an expensive trial, so they pay the settlement or, in this case, the ransom. I'm not really saying you shouldn't do it. It would be like saying don't make a website because you might get attacked by a hacker. It is just something I want you to be aware of. *Copyright* will protect your written or drawn idea, but it does not protect the spoken word. *Unregistered design right* is similar to copyright as in it is free, but it protects the outward appearance of the product.

This is all nice, but how effective is this in protecting your idea? Rarely anything is 100% effective. If you want to know how I think you should protect something you are close to developing: scream it from the top of your lungs. Put it out on the internet, on your website, social media… everywhere. 1 – there is no incentive stealing something that now everyone knows is yours and 2 – you may create big news with this approach if your product really is something great. And to be great it doesn't need to be revolutionary, it just needs to push the boundaries. But before you go out and start screaming you should have something to show for

120

it, not just an idea that didn't even have any time to mature. People still do like to copy products if they are good, but they will not be able to say that it was them who started this and imagined it.

But should you really be that careful about protecting your idea and allowing yourself to be scared that someone else will find out? NO! What is the worst thing that could happen if someone found out? Many men have shared their success stories, written books about it and how they came where they are now (or were) and became rich. Not 1% of the people who read those books followed in their footsteps because they were not ready to do the work that needed to be done and sacrifice what needed to be sacrificed. Everyone wants an easy way out. And this is not an easy business. And let's say your idea gets to that 0.3% who would act on it... So what? It is still your idea. Maybe that person knows your ingredient list for your products, but you know what is your brand personality, you know how you will present those products, you know their soul, while the other person has only the superficial stuff. And truthfully, to copy an idea is most compelling when the idea is a success.

When developing a Segway, a product its inventor thought would fly off the shelves in six months, he didn't get any feedback and went internally through several iterations because he was afraid someone would steal his idea. Sadly, even though he had some great inventions, this fear was the reason why this invention did not succeed. *Don't let the fear of losing your products be the reason you lose your products because you wouldn't talk to someone who may have been able to help you with your business.*

7 Prepare for the worst

I understand that this isn't the greatest title to come right after I tell you that you shouldn't give in to fear and not let fear control you. And I am not writing this as a pessimist or to talk you out of it, but it is something you need to know. The more you know, the better you can prepare for when you start your journey to your cosmetic line or some other line of business.

No business is easy. 90%, if not more, business start-ups fail. We could probably write books on top of books why new businesses fail, but we'll mention only a few things, so you get the idea. One of the reasons businesses fail is because *they fell in love with their own product*. These businesses are blinded by their subjective opinions of themselves, of their products, they are too obsessed about how great of an idea it all was and then reality check hits them. Sadly, too late. Another call for reality check is that they are *always too optimistic*. Tony Robbins puts this nicely when he says that too many people overestimate the first year and underestimate a decade. You will see new entrepreneurs throwing numbers about how large the market is and how much they plan to take and it works out in less than 10% of the cases. It is good to have structure in a company, but when first starting *you can't really segment everything*. Meaning that to get your company of the ground you will need to hustle and if needed you will not only be the CEO, but also the janitor. These are the two extremes, but don't be confided to only one role, you'll need to work to pull this off. If you can bypass these three things and apply the ones we spoke about earlier in the book, I strongly believe that you will be well on your way to be in the 10% and not the 90%.

But there is another reason why working with cosmetics is hard. When you're offering a service, you do the service and the person you did it for pays you. It's intellectual and you already have it available. When you're offering a physical product, unless someone is ordering a carving or a painting, you first need to have the product. That means you first need to spend money to get the item in order to sell the item. This becomes that much harder when you are also creating your own cosmetic line, because you're spending much more money. We spoke earlier about research and development, packaging, etc. You will have to pay for all of this before you can start, which is why having a cosmetic line isn't something that makes it on a top 10 list of businesses to start.

The journey isn't the easiest and you may have ups and downs, but if you're willing to work for what you want, then I have no doubt that you will succeed.

Conclusion

In conclusion, I believe we have covered here everything that you need to know to start working on your new cosmetic business, not only a cosmetic line. I am quite subjective here, I must admit, but I do believe this book brings a lot of value to the table for people who are just starting out and even for those who have already started, but may feel they are missing something. With all the elements it has and all the information it holds, even the quotes about success… It is written by someone just like you. I am not your distant number one publishing author who sold millions of copies teaching you how to write a book. I am not Elon Musk writing about how to start SpaceX. I am you after a period of very good and thorough research.

In the appendix you will find various things that may be of help to you, like tools for entrepreneurs and reading suggestions. I have always loved the Latin sayings and I personally place a lot of value in the quotes I have compiled here for you.

Also, I want to say that I am sorry for diluting the information that is specific to starting a cosmetic line, but I felt that it would benefit you too to know more about business in general, so that it is easier to do the things we usually don't see done behind the scenes. Robert Kiyosaki in his book „Rich dad, poor dad" mentions a business consultant that gave him the phrase: They are one skill away from great wealth. This is why I'm giving you all these tools. You may want to have a cosmetic line, but in order to have a successful one, you need more than just an e-mail of a laboratory.

Finally, I want to thank you for investing your time and money into reading this book and I hope that you have found it helpful and informative. I am usually a type of reader who doesn't like to write in the books or use markers, but if you happen to do it in one of mine, I'd love to see what you found important or what you liked. Apart from that type of review, I hope you will find the time in your busy day to also leave one on Amazon.

Welcome to being my competition.

Appendix

Quotes about success

1. Success is not final, failure is not fatal: it is the courage to continue that counts. – Winston S. Churchill
2. I can't give you a sure-fire formula for success, but I can give you a formula for failure: try to please everybody all the time. – Herbert Bayard Swope
3. Try not. Do or do not. – Yoda
4. Have no fear of perfection – you'll never reach it. – Salvador Dali
5. Success is stumbling from failure to failure with no loss of enthusiasm. – Winston Churchill
6. I'm a success today because I had a friend who believed in me and I didn't have the heart to let him down. – Abraham Lincoln
7. It is hard to fail, but it is worse never to have tried to succeed. – Theodore Roosevelt
8. Only those who dare to fail greatly can ever achieve greatly. – Robert F. Kennedy
9. Kites rise highest against the wind, not with it. – Winston S. Churchill
10. Whatever the mind can conceive and believe, it can achieve. – Napoleon Hill
11. Rich people have small TVs and big libraries, and poor people have small libraries and big TVs. – Zig Ziglar
12. Well done is better than well said. – Benjamin Franklin
13. Eighty percent of success is showing up. – Woody Allen
14. Curious that we spend more time congratulating people who have succeeded than encouraging people who have not. – Neil deGrasse Tyson
15. People rarely succeed unless they have fun in what they are doing. – Dale Carnegie
16. Success is not the key to happiness. Happiness is the key to success. If you love what you are doing, you will be successful. – Herman Cain
17. Don't wait. The time will never be just right. – Napoleon Hill
18. Doing the best at this moment puts you in the best place for the next moment. – Oprah Winfrey
19. Nothing in the world can take the place of perseverance. Talent will not; nothing is more common than unsuccessful people with talent. Genius will not; unrewarded genius is almost legendary. Education will not; the world is full of educated derelicts. Perseverance and determination alone are omnipotent. – Calvin Coolidge
20. Start where you are. Use what you have. Do what you can. – Arthur Ashe
21. Your attitude, not your aptitude, will determine your altitude. – Zig Ziglar
22. The road to success is always under construction. – Lily Tomlin

23. I find that the harder I work, the more luck I seem to have. – Thomas Jefferson
24. Striving for success without hard work is like trying to harvest where you haven't planted. – David Bly
25. The best revenge is massive success. – Frank Sinatra
26. You may be disappointed if you fail, but you are doomed if you don't try. – Beverly Sills
27. The roughest roads often lead to the top. – Christina Aguilera
28. The road to success is dotted with many tempting parking spaces. – Will Rogers
29. There's no reason to have a plan B because it distracts from plan A. – Will Smith
30. If you really want the key to success, start by doing the opposite of what everyone else is doing. – Brad Szollose
31. Don't be afraid to give up the good to go for the great. – John D. Rockefeller
32. If you want to be successful, it's just this simple. Know what you are doing. Love what you are doing. And believe in what you are doing. – Will Rogers
33. When you go in search of honey, you must expect to be stung by bees. – Joseph Joubert
34. Once you figure out what you want in life – expect nothing less. – Lorii Myers
35. Timing, perseverance, and ten years of trying will eventually make you look like an overnight success. – Biz Stone
36. That some achieve great success, is proof to all that others can achieve it as well. – Abraham Lincoln
37. Don't dare to dream big, just dream BIG! – Stephen Richards
38. A man who fails well is greater than one who succeeds badly. – Thomas Merton
39. Success shuns the man who lacks ideas. – David J. Schwartz
40. Strive to enrich all lives, hearts and minds not just your own pockets. – Rasheed Ogunlaru
41. Identify your problems but give your power and energy to solutions. – Tony Robbins
42. When your life flashes before your eyes, make sure you've got plenty to watch. – Anonymous
43. A friendship founded on business is a good deal better than a business founded on friendship. – John D. Rockefeller
44. An entrepreneur is someone who jumps off a cliff and builds a plane on the way down. – Reid Hoffman
45. The trick to succeeding is to stop thinking that there's a trick to everything. – Robert Brault
46. Those who have succeeded at anything and don't mention luck are kidding themselves. – Larry King

47. Success is more permanent when you achieve it without destroying your principles. – Walter Cronkite
48. The closer one gets to the top, the more one finds there is no "top". – Nancy Barcus
49. Success is 99 percent failure. – Soichiro Honda
50. Success is to be measured not so much by the position that one has reached in life as by the obstacles which he has overcome. – Booker T. Washington
51. It had long since come to my attention that people of accomplishment rarely sat back and let things happen to them. They went out and happened to things. – Leonardo da Vinci
52. A man is a success if he gets up in the morning and gets to bed at night, and in between he does what he wants to do. – Bob Dylan
53. You will find the key to success under the alarm clock. – Benjamin Franklin
54. Success is simply a matter of luck. Ask any failure. – Earl Wilson
55. Success is a lousy teacher. It seduces smart people into thinking they can't lose. – Bill Gates
56. I do not try to be anyone's savior. I only try to think about the future and not be sad. – Elon Musk
57. If you're going through hell, keep going. – Winston Churchill
58. If you are influenced by the opinion of others, you will have no desire of your own. – Napoleon Hill
59. If information is a tool, misinformation is a weapon. - Unknown
60. Tell the world what you intend to do, but first show it. – Napoleon Hill
61. Formal education will make you a living, self education will make you a fortune. – Jim Rohn
62. People often say that motivation doesn't last. Well, neither does bathing. That's why we recommend it daily. – Zig Ziglar
63. Our greatest weakness lies in giving up. – Thomas A. Edison
64. You don't have to be great to start, but you have to start to be great. – Zig Ziglar
65. If opportunity doesn't knock, build a door. – Milton Berle
66. I've learned so much from my mistakes. I'm thinking of making a few more. – Cheryl Cole
67. Normality is a paved road. It's comfortable to walk, but no flowers grow on it. – Vincent van Gogh
68. The reason we struggle with insecurity is because we compare our behind-the-scenes with everyone else's highlight reel. – Steve Furtick
69. Losers quit when they fail. Winners fail until they succeed. – Robert Kiyosaki
70. Life isn't about finding yourself. Life is about creating yourself. – George Bernard Shaw
71. A problem is a chance for you to do your best. – Duke Ellington

72. When everything seems to be going against you remember that the plain takes off against the wind, not with it. – Henry Ford.

73. One of the very worst uses of time is to do something very well that need not be done at all. – Brian Tracy

74. Everyone procrastinates. The difference between high performers and low performers is largely determined by what they choose to procrastinate on. – Brian Tracy

75. No matter what the level of your ability, you have more potential than you can ever develop in a lifetime. – James T. McCay

76. A journey of a thousand leagues begins with a single step. – Lao-Tsu

77. Anytime you stop trying to get better you're bound to get worse. – Pat Riley

78. Effort can be its own reward, if you let it. – Seth Godin

79. Life is a series of mentors. – Daymond John

80. The person who invented the ship also invented the shipwreck. – Seth Godin

81. If somebody offers you an amazing opportunity but you are not sure you can do it, say yes – then learn how to do it later. – Sir Richard Branson

82. When something is important enough you do it even if the odds aren't in your favor. – Elon Musk

83. Most of the important things in the world have been accomplished by people who have kept on trying when there seemed to be no hope at all. – Dale Carnegie

84. Immerse yourself in the energy of what you desire. – Hiro Boga

85. The components make an entrepreneur: the person, the idea and the resources to make it happen. – Anita Roddick

86. Whatever you can do, or dream you can do, begin it. Boldness has genius, power and magic in it. Begin it now. – Johan Wolfgang von Goethe

87. Everything you want is on the other side of fear. – Jack Canfield

88. Tend to the people and they will tend to the business. – John Maxwell

89. I've missed more than 9000 shots in my career. I've lost almost 300 games. Twenty-six times I've been trusted to take the game winning shot and missed. I've failed over and over and over again in my life. And that is why I succeed. – Michael Jordan

90. Change before you have to. – Jack Welch

91. If you aren't in over your head, how do you know how tall you are? – T.S. Eliot

92. When they say you can't, they show you their limits, not your. – Kevin Keenoo

93. Failure only occurs if you are not learning. – Guy Kawasaki

94. I am always doing that which I cannot do, in order that I may learn how to do it. – Pablo Picaso

95. Don't be afraid to take a big step. You can't cross a chasm in two small jumps. – David Lloyd George

96. Two roads diverged in a wood... I took the one less traveled by, and that has made all the difference. – Robert Frost

97. It is not the critic who counts; not the man who points out how the strong man stumbles, or where the doer of deeds could have done them better. The credit belongs to the man who is actually in the arena, whose face is marred by dust and sweat and blood; who strives valiantly; who errs, who comes short again and again, who at the best knows in the end the triumph of high achievement, and who, at the worst, if he fails, at least fails while daring greatly. – Theodore Roosevelt

98. The best businesses begin with empathy. – Brian Solis

99. The most destructive force in the universe... is regret. – Tomy Lee Jones as Agent K, Men in Black 3

100. If you think you're too small to have an impact, try going to bed with a mosquito. – Anita Roddick

101. Next to doing the right thing, the most important thing is letting people know you are doing the right thing. – John D. Rockefeller

102. Don't spend any money until you make some. – Noah Kagan

103. You'll never be anything if you think the glass is half full. If you want to be anything, walk in the room and ask why isn't that glass full. – Jim Jefferies.

104. Nobody will ever pay you to solve your problems, but they will line up if you can solve theirs. – Unknown

105. You spend time with people that don't do something, you start feeling like you can't do it. – Unknown

106. We have met the enemy and he is us. – Pogo

107. Try never to be the smartest person in the room. And if you are, I suggest you invite smarter people... or find a different room. – Michael Dell

108. My experience has taught me that a man is never quite so near success as when that which he calls 'failure' has overtaken him, for it is on occasions of this sort that he is forced to think. If he thinks accurately, and with persistence, he discovers that so-called failure usually is nothing more than a signal to re-arm himself with a new plan or purpose. Most real failures are due to limitations which men set up in their own minds. If they had the courage to go one step further, they would discover their error. – Andrew Carnegie

109. Perfection is the enemy of done. – Unknown

Your statement

Here I want you to write your statement, your motivation to start a business, give the force that is driving you words and read it every day and night as you were to convince yourself of it. When you write down a goal it gets a form, otherwise it's just a fantasy. Give your goal a deadline.

_____
_____
_____
_____
_____
_____
_____
_____
_____
_____
_____
_____
_____
_____
_____
_____
_____
_____
_____
_____
_____
_____

Websites for a modern day entrepreneur

http://www.startupcompanylawyer.com/
It is probably best if you could hire one, but if you do not have the budget to do that right away, maybe this is a good place to start and see if there is anything that helps you mitigate risks in the legal sense.

http://www.docracy.com/
Docracy is a website that has various templates of legal documents for you, to help you with founding a company, running a small business, having a model release, etc.

https://www.javelin.com/beta
Javelin lets you test your idea on customer and try to measure if they will respond good or bad and with that feedback adjust for a better result.

http://bit.do/
There are other websites that will allow you to shorten links, but here you will be able to also customize the links for free.

https://www.prlog.org/
PR log is a web-tool that allows you to post your press release and have it indexed, hosted and distributed to search engines.

http://www.stumbleupon.com
This is a website that will let you submit your own links to it and people will be able to stumble upon them by shuffling through it. You stay on one page until you click 'stumble' and then you go to the next one.

https://www.reddit.com/
Reddit is a website similar to stumble upon, but instead of the website shuffling content for you, you are the one responsible for clicking around and finding the topics and content that is interesting for you to follow. Add your content to the topic carefully, so people can find it in threads related to you.

https://www.linkedin.com/
LinkedIn is a great social site for business people and people who are in the prospect becoming one or looking to get in touch or follow some.

https://mailtrack.io/en/

As the name suggests, mailtrack is a plug-in for G-Mail that will help you track the activity of your e-mail. If they are read, how long until it was opened and the PRO versions have more data you could play with.

https://signature-maker.net/

Signature Maker is a curious and funny little tool that basically lets you to use the pen tool to hand write your own name on the screen for a digital signature. Unless you have a stylus, you'll need to do this with a mouse, it doesn't look pretty.

http://invoiceto.me/ and https://www.free-invoice-generator.com/

Invoicely and free invoice generator are great tools when you want to at least appear more serious and itemize your goods and services to the people or companies you have worked with.

https://www.waveapps.com/

Wave is a little bit bigger tool than the previous two and is helping small businesses not only do invoices, but accounting as a whole. Great tool to use.

https://www.grammarly.com/l

One of the important things in business is to not have your correspondence with a business prospect full of grammar mistakes. It can be added to Chrome, Windows and Microsoft Office. You should write *grammarly* correct.

http://www.hemingwayapp.com/

While grammarly is focused on your writing being grammatically correct, Hemingway will grade your text to some other standards. The text is graded by complexity of the sentences, use of overcomplicated words when there are simpler ones (it recognizes the words, but you may not be able to use the alternatives in the context you need them), adverbs, passive voice.

https://trends.google.com/trends and https://www.google.com/analytics/#

Google Trends are good for following the current trends for almost any kind of entrepreneur, writer, creative, content creator… Google analytics is a great tool for understanding visitor traffic to your website.

https://adwords.google.com/home/

Google addwords can help you understand what the users are searching and start a pay per click advertising campaign on Google.

https://www.cyfe.com/

Cyfe claims to be an all-in-one business dashboard. But I did not notice it offer anything you can't do anywhere else. So at this point it's only your preference of what you want to use.

https://moz.com/researchtools/ose/

After you enter your domain this website will give you a breakdown of some key facts about your website, including your domain authority, page authority and how many links you have pointing to your website.

https://mailchimp.com/

Mail Chimp lets you send 12,000 e-mails to 2,000 contacts. Using a third party like this is good because if you use an e-mail from your website it can often be recognized as spam. Even the ones like Yahoo and Gmail can fall under this if you send too many e-mails. It can even integrate with Google Analytics directly.

https://wetransfer.com/

We're moving forward in technology, but somehow attachments are going forward as much as cell phone batteries – they aren't. Sometimes you need to send files that are larger than the usual 20 MB or so. This is a great website if you need to e-mail someone file up to 2 GB in size for free.

https://www.dropbox.com/

Similar to WeTransfer, Dropbox is also a file sharing system, with a small difference. While WeTransfer is an alternative to e-mail, Dropbox is also a file keeping system, a storage which can be upgraded, to which you can grant people access and share it among your team.

https://mixpanel.com/

Product analytics for product people, deeply understand every user's journey with instant insights for everyone on mobile and web is how Mixpanel describes itself.

https://www.marketingevolution.com/

Marketing Evolution is helpful for making Return On Investment plans and results. It helps you figure out in real-time which marketing efforts you are doing work best with different types of people and situations and have best ROI.

https://www.kwanko.com/en

Kwanko is one of the leading actors in multi-channel advertising. By working closely with top brands and worldwide advertising agencies, the group has acquired a solid reputation and extensive background in Performance Advertising.

https://www.hellobar.com/ and http://optinmonster.com/

These are tools used to create the pop-out advertising on a website that appear once it registers your mouse moving towards the outside of the body of the site, which is usually a sign that you are about to close it. I find these annoying, but it seems that some have used them effectively to convert visitors.

https://wordpress.org/plugins/social-locker/

When speaking about the features I don't like, we can mention this one too. I am not a fan of it, but that doesn't mean you can't utilize it. A plug-in called social locker is locking your content behind a request for a like, share, tweet, etc.

https://business.linkedin.com/sales-solutions/compare-plans/sales-navigator-for-gmail# or https://business.linkedin.com/sales-solutions/sales-navigator

We spoke about Chrome before. Rapportive and Sales Navigator are extensions installed on Chrome for Gmail, which recognizes the e-mail and links it to a LinkedIn profile for you.

Some other logical ones if you want to follow entrepreneurship and business related news would be

1. https://www.entrepreneur.com/
2. https://www.inc.com/
3. http://fortune.com/
4. https://www.entrepreneurship.org/
5. https://www.bloomberg.com/
6. https://www.wsj.com/news/business
7. http://www.success.com/
8. http://www.barrons.com/
9. https://hbr.org/
10. http://www.adweek.com/
11. https://www.ted.com/
12. https://www.sba.gov/business-guide/

Websites dedicated to cosmetics

If you want to learn more about the world of cosmetics, these are some of the websites that you should probably visit and see if they offer something for you too. On these websites you can find out more about some ingredients and why they are avoided, like parabens and sulfates, you can find out about getting jobs in the cosmetic industry, working as a consultant, finding raw materials and laboratories, etc.

Also, please keep in mind that I did not extensively test these websites and because of my lack of expertise in that field I cannot vouch for them, even if they may be the best in their field, but I do use some of these websites and I can say that they are at least a good starting point for anyone interested in cosmetics.

https://www.fdanews.com/
If you are located in the USA or plan to place your products there, even if it may not contain too much information about cosmetics, you may want to follow this for notifications about eventual changes in the field.

http://www.cosmeticsandtoiletries.com/
As part of the Cosmetics & Toiletries (C&T) brand, Cosmetics and Toiletries was created for professional cosmetic R&D staff, specifically cosmetic chemists, product formulators, research scientists and R&D managers developing and manufacturing cosmetic and personal care products.

http://www.gcimagazine.com/
Global Cosmetic Industry magazine is one that can easily find itself in the previous collection of websites, since it's about business and marketing, but also covers some topics like personal care, fragrance, etc.

http://www.eurocosmetics-magazine.com/
EURO COSMETICS is a trade journal for the cosmetics and fragrance industry that has been recognized for decades and that enjoys worldwide circulation; it is admired internationally for being extremely informative. EURO COSMETICS is published in German and English 10 times per year in print edition, e-paper, pdf edition.

http://www.scconline.org/journal-of-cosmetic-science/

Journal of the Society of Cosmetic Chemists publishes technical papers on topics of interest to cosmetic scientists and is distributed six times per year, accessed exclusively by SCC Members. Yearly Membership in the Society of Cosmetic Chemists includes printed volumes of the Journal of Cosmetic Science. In addition, members have access to the online Journal and Journal archives dating back to 1947.

https://www.omicsonline.org/cosmetology-trichology.php

Journal of Cosmetology & Trichology is an open access, Peer reviewed journal. The Journal of Cosmetology and Trichology collects data from reliable source of information on discoveries and current developments as original article, review articles, case reports, short communications, etc. It consists of the information about the new inventions and the use of different cosmetics.

http://www.happi.com/

HAPPI is the leading media outlet in the global personal care and household product market. Celebrating 50 years of global coverage in 2013, Happi provides in-depth analysis of this $530 billion market for 16,500 subscribers around the world.

http://www.perfumerflavorist.com/

Perfumer & Flavorist magazine brings more than a century of expertise to the latest insights in formulation and applications, raw materials (aroma chemicals, essential oils, flavor ingredients, extracts, spices), and other natural and synthetic materials, technological breakthroughs, trends and more.

https://www.cosmeticsbusiness.com/

Cosmetics Business is part of HPCi media and also covers business in cosmetics, like what are the trends in different markets, expansions of some companies, etc. They also have news about regulatory trends in cosmetic business.

http://www.mdedge.com/edermatologynews

Dermatology News Digital Network is the online destination and multimedia properties of Dermatology News, the independent news publication for the dermatology community. Since 1970, Dermatology News has been the leading source of news and commentary about clinical developments in dermatology as well as health care policy and regulations that affect the physician's practice. Dermatology News Digital Network is owned by Frontline Medical Communications.

https://www.aad.org/
The American Academy of Dermatology was founded in 1938. It is the largest, most influential and representative dermatology group in the United States. With a membership of more than 19,000, it represents virtually all practicing dermatologists in the United States, as well as a growing number of international dermatologists.

https://www.cosmeticseurope.eu/
Cosmetics Europe is the European trade association for the cosmetics and personal care industry. The members include cosmetics and personal care manufacturers, and also associations representing the industry at national level, right across Europe. Directly, or through the national membership, Cosmetics Europe represents over 4,500 innovative companies.

For some of the other websites from the field you can visit the FDA website and see their list here[57].

---

[57] https://www.fda.gov/Cosmetics/ResourcesForYou/Industry/ucm077674.htm

Reading suggestions

Think and Grow Rich by Napoleon Hill
Napoleon Hill is probably the grandfather of business self development books and personal growth. It is filled with life lessons of various business people of his time and some before him and he puts a great value in faith, determination, desire – that you attract what you wish the most. It is a great read, but I'd still suggest you skip chapter XI, the mystery of sex transmutation. Not sure about you, but the last thing I want to read about in a book about business is sex.

Eat that frog! by Brian Tracy
No, this is not a book about how to be French. This is a book about how to stop procrastinating and get more done in less time. It also teaches us about creative procrastination. Basically, it suggest that we do the worst thing first and then everything else will follow easier.

Fail Fast or Win Big by Bernhard Schroeder
There are two main part to this book, business plan and crowdfunding. Both are very much informative and useful. Bernhard also adds some of the entrepreneur stories at the end of each chapter called entrepreneur insight and some key takeaways. Unlike some of the books I read that were almost only a collection of stories about people who made it, this is a book that only uses those as an examples and to add even more value to an already good book.

The 22 immutable laws of marketing by Al Ries and Jack Trout
A very thin, concise and to the point book about marketing. First published in 1994 the commonsense wisdom still applies to most of the principles even today.

The 22 immutable laws of branding (with The 11 immutable laws of internet branding) by Al Ries and Laura Ries
The immutability of the laws, which the authors admit they chose for sounding better, falls in the water when they stress Yahoo! as a winner in the search engine group because it was a first mover. You can't help but giggle while thinking of Google. That being said, it's not a bad book at all, you will find some useful information here about choosing a name that is short, simple, alliterative, suggest a category, etc.

The E Myth Revisited by Michael E. Gerber

I like the book because it appeals to both sides of a medal, you might say. It is a book about business, but it is not written like a cookbook, with recipes to success. It is not telling us what to do or talking directly to you, but it is almost like a novel, conversing with a business owner and letting you come to your own conclusions. If you're anywhere near emotional there are some revelations that main character Sarah discovers, that could almost make you cry.

Zero to One, notes on startups, or how to build the future by Peter Thiel

This isn't a book that will teach you many new things on the topic you are interested in, but it is nonetheless insightful, thought provoking and enlightening. Peter tells us that we are not a lottery ticket. Many successful people now like to say that they were lucky, but behind that luck was a lot more work, sweat and tears.

Perennial Seller: The Art of Making and Marketing Work that Lasts by Ryan Holiday

In this book Ryan analyzes what it takes to be in for a long haul. He does this by questioning your motives, how much time you should spend on what, several marketing techniques, etc. This book is mostly about being an author and writing a book, but the strategies and, more importantly, the thinking behind them is still universal and applies to whatever you need them to apply to. Reading the book I found that we followed some of the same people and used the same quotes, so it's just natural when I say that I like the way that it was written.

Rich dad, poor dad by Robert Kiyosaki

This is a book where Robert talks about his two dads. One was his biological dad who has always pushed him to be good at school and the other one was his friends dad who taught him about financial literacy and business, a person who dropped out of school, but still ended up running companies and people who finished school out of fear and desire in the search for wealth answered to him. In his book Robert shows why the rich get richer and poor get poorer. It is written in a narrative about two boys learning financial literacy, but still direct enough that you do not need to search for the meaning.

Jab, jab, jab, right hook by Gary Vaynerchuk

In this book Gary shares his knowledge of the social networks and how to share content more natively for each and every one of them, giving you examples of what is good and what is bad. The book is a little older and some platforms have added some features, but the core principles still stand.

The Art of non-conformity by Chris Guillebeau

In this book Chris challenges us to not be contempt with the way people tell us we should live, learn or work. He challenges all those things. He skipped high school and went to college, traveled all the countries in the world and is living the life he wants and likes to. He refers to his masters degree as a $32,000 lesson in motivation, but doesn't dismiss school completely. All in all, a decent book on how not to become one of the monkeys he mentions. One could say that Chris is living the words of Erich Fromm when he said that "Modern man lives under the illusion that he knows what he wants, while he actually wants what he is supposed to want".

There are a lot of books out there on entrepreneurship, as well as countless seminars you can attend. Not one of them will make you an entrepreneur. If you want to be an entrepreneur, be one.

Fail Fast or Win Big
Bernhard Schroeder

Still round the corner there may wait
A new road or a secret gate,
And though we pass them by today,
Tomorrow we may come this way
And take the hidden paths that run
Towards the Moon or to the Sun.

Lord of the Rings
J.R.R. Tolkien

https://www.linkedin.com/in/davorpavlic/

@davorpavlich

@pavlicdavor

https://www.facebook.com/davor.d.davor

http://bit.ly/davorpavlicyoutube

dpavlic24

www.ingramcontent.com/pod-product-compliance
Lightning Source LLC
Chambersburg PA
CBHW081727220526
45468CB00008B/2005